CRACKING THE INNOVATION CODE

Author Dr Andy Wynn, along with contributions from leaders of some of the biggest companies on the planet (including DuPont, 3M, Johnson Matthey and Imerys), finally reveals the secret of how you can unlock the potential in your business to grow.

In the follow-up to his book *Transforming Technology into Profit*, Andy takes you on a journey that explains how the organisation and culture within your business impact your company's ability to innovate.

Using his "Three Tiers of Successful Innovation", Andy reveals how to clearly identify what aspects of your business are holding back growth and how to use that information to transform your business into one that facilitates growth by revitalising the structure and culture of your business to focus employee behaviours on adding profitable new revenue streams.

Part sequel and part companion volume to his previous book, Andy finally "cracks the code" on how to unleash your business' ability to create and successfully commercialise new products.

Written in the author's trademark conversational style, *Cracking the Innovation Code* offers a refreshingly practical and real-world view, written by someone who has been there and done it, and enhanced by valuable case studies and contributions from numerous senior executives who have made lifelong careers out of leading innovation, and with a passion for leading industrial manufacturing businesses.

Andy Wynn is the former CTO at a billion-dollar multinational manufacturer, with over 30 years' experience of delivering business growth through new technologies, all over the world. He is the founder of TTIP Consulting, the Strategic Innovation Company, and author of the books *Transforming Technology into Profit* and *The Biggest City You've Never Heard Of*.

"Part memoir and lessons learned, part 'how to' guide. In *Cracking the Innovation Code*, Andy Wynn provides a framework for identifying and resolving the 'internal factors' holding your organization back from realizing maximum revenue growth from R&D investments. A cross functional view is taken from idea generation through commercialization of new products. It will be the first book I hand to new leaders so that they can take a short cut to what took me 20 years to learn."

—Philip Clark, Global Technical Director, Automotive and Aerospace Division, 3M

"Most books in this space only focus on the theories behind innovation, or how to generate new ideas, but don't address the practical realities of how to actually ensure the continuous delivery of innovation in a business. This book states clearly what the challenges are and how to overcome them."

—Maurits van Tol, Chief Technology Officer, Johnson Matthey plc

"The author's latest book is once again a pragmatic reinforcement that successful businesses not only foster a culture of innovation, but also have strong processes and checks in place to ensure successful new product development and deployment. A great read."

—Dominic Greensmith, President of Advanced Technology Group, DPS Engineering

"There are so many books on innovation out there it's confusing where to start, *Cracking the Innovation Code* sweeps all that aside and tells you like it is, no fancy jargon, no 'get rich quick' schemes, just practical business truths. Refreshing to see some honesty in this genre for a change."

—Robert Park, Managing Director, TPPS Investment Casting Ltd

"Whether you are a business leader or a technologist, Dr Wynn explains clearly how to navigate the complex world of innovation to generate real results."

—Peter Davies, Chief Executive, James Lister & Sons Limited

"*Cracking the Innovation Code* is a practical guide for the way companies should look at how to grow their business. This book is about putting all the theory you read about into practice, in the real world, and it works!"

—Mike Murray, Chief Technology Officer, The Vita Group

CRACKING THE INNOVATION CODE

How to Unlock the True Potential of Your Business to Grow Through New Products

Andy Wynn

Routledge
Taylor & Francis Group
LONDON AND NEW YORK

First published 2021
by Routledge
2 Park Square, Milton Park, Abingdon, Oxon OX14 4RN

and by Routledge
52 Vanderbilt Avenue, New York, NY 10017

Routledge is an imprint of the Taylor & Francis Group, an informa business

British Library Cataloguing-in-Publication Data
A catalogue record for this book is available from the British Library

Library of Congress Cataloging-in-Publication Data
Names: Wynn, Andrew, 1965- author.
Title: Cracking the innovation code: how to unlock the true potential of your business to grow through new products / Andy Wynn.
Description: Abingdon, Oxon; New York, NY: Routledge, 2021. | Includes bibliographical references.
Identifiers: LCCN 2020024934 (print) | LCCN 2020024935 (ebook) | ISBN 9780367566548 (hbk) | ISBN 9780367567118 (pbk) | ISBN 9781003099086 (ebk)
Subjects: LCSH: Creative ability in business. | Organizational change. | Technological innovations. | Strategic planning.
Classification: LCC HD53 .W95 2021 (print) | LCC HD53 (ebook) | DDC 658.5/75–dc23
LC record available at https://lccn.loc.gov/2020024934
LC ebook record available at https://lccn.loc.gov/2020024935

ISBN: 978-0-367-56654-8 (hbk)
ISBN: 978-0-367-56711-8 (pbk)
ISBN: 978-1-003-09908-6 (ebk)

Typeset in Joanna
by Deanta Global Publishing Services, Chennai, India

CONTENTS

PREFACE

Cracking the Innovation Code is the third book I've written in just over a year, so people inevitably comment, "Wow, you're pumping them out now", or "You're really on a roll". And I can't say what the secret is, but it's definitely something to do with moving to Spain and the positive change in lifestyle that brings. I'm sure the 330 days a year of sunshine are a big factor. One thing I have certainly learnt living here is, "When the Marbella Muse hits, you can't ignore her", so keep writing.

And what's maybe more remarkable is that I've written all three books on my last-generation Sony Vaio laptop, which I have been clinging on to for dear life until the bitter end. The shift key has split, the letter "E" has dropped off three times and I've had to glue it back in (try writing a book without the letter "E"!), the "Pg Dn" key has dropped off twice and still doesn't fit back in the keyboard correctly and lately, the letter "S" has taken to dropping out now and again. Also, the screen occasionally goes haywire on booting up, so I know it's only a matter of time before it stops working permanently. I have always had Sony Vaios as my laptop of choice throughout their brand lifecycle, but as they have stopped making them now, and I have typed this last one into the ground, now that I've finished book number three, I'm definitely going to reward myself in the New Year with a new device.

Andy Wynn
Marbella, Spain
January 2020

ACKNOWLEDGEMENTS

None of this would have been possible without all of the team at TTIP Consulting, and all of our customers and business partners. Thanks for all your support (which has kept me going), all the great conversations (which frequently cause me to stop and think) and for keeping my passion for "transforming technology into profit" alive.

Many of the case studies discussed in this book are from long years back in my early career. None of the projects were done alone, and I would particularly like to thank all of the team members I worked with during my early days as a Technology Director on the projects discussed in Chapter 3, including Basant Agarwal, Nashim Imam, Mark Gittus, Matt Stanyer and Tam Padley.

I would like to thank a number of academic experts in innovation and entrepreneurship that I have had the pleasure to discuss some of my ideas with during the writing of this book, including Professors James Hayton, Giuliana Battisti and Joe Haslam.

A particular thanks to a number of key contributors, including Ian Sterritt, Cliff Spiro, Maurits van Tol, Chris Parr, Phil Clark and Alexa Dembek, who all contributed important insights and case studies that enriched this book considerably.

And as always, I would like to thank my wife, Julie, who continues to be the real secret of all my success.

ABOUT THE AUTHOR

Dr Andy Wynn is an international business leader and former CTO at a billion-dollar FTSE 250 multinational manufacturer, with over 30 years' experience of delivering business growth through new technologies and realigning business and innovation strategies for industrial and high-tech companies all over the world.

His career long passion has been "transforming technology into profit", creating new technologies and building new businesses from them. Following the publication of his first book *Transforming Technology into Profit: A Guide to Leading New Ideas through the Complexities of the Corporate World and Transforming Them into Successful New Products*, Andy launched TTIP Consulting, an international consulting firm that helps industrial and high-tech businesses unlock their potential for growth through innovation. More information can be found at www.ttipconsulting.com.

A seasoned world traveller and global citizen, Andy's career has taken him all over the world, working in North and South America, throughout Europe, the Middle East and right across Asia and Australia. He has a particular passion for China, having spent 20 years regularly travelling and doing business there, including over six years living there. His time in China became a life-changing period and motivated him to publish his second book *The Biggest City You've Never Heard Of: A Story of Personal Growth through the Challenges of Life in Modern Day China*.

Andy is a regular speaker at conferences, industry events and business schools on the subjects of "How to Unlock Innovation in Business" and "Doing Business in China".

In his spare time, Andy is very active and spends much of his free time in the gym or outdoors. He spent 17 years studying kung fu and has a black belt and is a licensed instructor. As middle age and injuries began to take their toll, he swapped kung fu for tennis and has been playing regularly for several years now.

He is an accomplished musician and singer and has been playing electric guitar since he was 16. His album *Never Too Late* was released on Office Records in 2012, and is available on iTunes, Amazon and many other digital media outlets.

Andy now lives in Marbella, Spain with his wife Julie, who is a talented painter.

INTRODUCTION

In my previous book, *Transforming Technology into Profit: A Guide to Leading New Ideas through the Complexities of the Corporate World and Transforming Them into Successful New Products* (ISBN: 9781792736858), I explored the process of innovation in businesses in some detail, delving into the key steps that companies have to go through in order to generate ideas, sift through them to identify those with the potential for commercial benefit and then convert them into saleable products. At the same time, I explored a long list of the practical barriers that can and do come along to wreak havoc on the innovation process, holding back business growth, mostly built around the themes of "people, politics and process". But in exploring these themes, I made certain to set them all within the context of a real business, with real people, and hinted in the book at the role that organisation and culture play in setting the real world business context within which innovation has to play. In this, my new book, *Cracking the Innovation Code*, I take these concepts further and explore just how huge an influence organisation and culture have on a business's ability to "transform technology into profit", and how you can take steps to identify the pain points and work to debottleneck them. So, this latest book builds on the first, and really takes a holistic look under the hood of a business, how the moving parts interact and seeing where things can go truly wrong when a business wants to grow through new products.

That's what we're going to explore over the next 200 pages. But first, let's go back a step and start by exploring the concept of "innovation" itself.

I really have to start by apologising for the use of the "I" word so often in this book, because in recent years, "innovation" has become one of the latest business buzzwords, part of the latest management speak. Almost every other conference these days seems to have the word "innovation" in the title. The internet is littered with articles, websites, podcasts, blogs and numerous other forums dedicated to one aspect or another of innovation. It has recently permeated almost every sector of business. The global spread and overuse of the word "innovation" has got so extensive now, that it's right up there with that other overused buzzword, "disruption". It has got to the point now, that often, whenever I mention "innovation" to people in business, they just roll their eyes, which then glaze over. You can almost hear their brain groaning and them thinking, "Oh no, here we go again, more consultant speak!"

Because of its proliferation in so many sectors of business, the word "innovation" has come to mean different things to different industries. To some businesses, it means creating new business models (Strategyzer has built a whole business out of this); to others, it means turning basic science into useful technology and products; to others it means the process of creative idea generation; and to yet others it means a more generalised process of improving many aspects of running a business, including business processes, distribution channels, value chains, etc. There are numerous businesses and public organisations now that have jobs on their staff with "innovation" in their title: innovation officer, innovation manager, innovation director, chief innovation officer, and the like, all doing seemingly different things depending on the type of business. There are even companies out there claiming to solve all your innovation needs with their new "innovation" management software. Innovation gets linked to digital transformation, it gets used in conjunction with Industry 4.0 and I've even seen an "Innovation in Music" conference (and why not? It sounds fun).

One of the most recent trends I have experienced in this whole new multifaceted industry of "innovation", is in the use of the term with reference to exploring new business models. I have listened to plenty of management consultants at conferences, in networking forums and on social media, stressing that the most profitable form of innovation is business model innovation, usually followed up with a few numbers to back up their statements.

All to make the case that it is far more profitable to reinvent (or "innovate") your business model than it is to develop better products in your existing business. And sure, I don't disagree. If you can truly identify a better business model and pivot your whole organisation towards this, then yes, the rewards can be outstanding. But what they don't dwell on is that in order to practically achieve such a monumental change to your business, you are taking a massive risk and you are going to suck up a huge amount of your resources trying to make it happen. And even if you do achieve the tremendous task of identifying and implementing a better business model, what are you left with? You still have a business, albeit a different style of business, so you still have products, you still have customers, you still have competitors. So you still need to keep developing new and improved products to stay ahead of those competitors, to gain better traction with your customers and to grow your market share and profit. So it all still boils down to product innovation, whichever way you look at it. New product development innovation is a fundamental set of skills and processes that every single business needs to capture and drive effectively in order to maintain profit generation, market leadership and achieve the growth they all strive for.

All these "innovation" meanings are of course valid in the strict definition of the word, but as a concept for business, it does not help that all these different usages result in "innovation" meaning different things to different people. So I'm not saying it's technically wrong, but I am saying it's confusing people. In essence, "innovation" as a business concept has become diluted. Its use in so many different contexts has created ambiguity and confusion, and this is why it has started to cause some to roll their eyes whenever it's mentioned. And all of this is pretty ironic, because one of the biggest barriers to innovation is jargon, the use of terminology that lacks shared meaning and therefore lacks clarity, ambiguous terms that can mean different things to different people. And so, "innovation" has actually become its own barrier in today's business world, as too many people ride the latest wave in business speak. A whole industry has grown up around providing innovation services, advice and academic analysis, and one which has built its own vocabulary and language, and you will regularly hear people lost in this world talking about disruption, lean start-ups, incubators, accelerators, agile, etc, etc.

But of course, it's not like we didn't have innovation in the past. It's not like we didn't do all this in the "good old days". It's not like this latest generation has invented innovation – business has always thrived on it. The evidence is all around us. Our economies would not be the same without it. Our lives would not be the same if the previous generations had not constantly innovated. Back in the day, we just had different words for all these things. The more generalised process of improving all aspects of running a business that has become labelled with the "innovation" tag, we used to call "continuous improvement", and very successful people were at it: reducing rejects in production processes, streamlining sales processes, minimising lost time accidents, all done without the management speak label of innovation. So why has "innovation" become such a bandwagon that so many people have jumped on?

In my day, innovation meant one thing, turning basic science into practical useful technology. And in a business context this meant "new product development", creating new products to satisfy new and evolving customer needs, new products that added new, profitable revenue streams to deliver business growth. Innovation meant new technologies and new designs, it meant merging technologies together to make new products, with new functionalities, and using your technologies in new applications. Back in my day, when you thought about innovation, you thought of the iPhone, you thought of Dyson, you thought of electric vehicles, you thought of 3D printing, of robots in the workplace. All these things, and thousands of other exciting new technologies are the result of basic science being transformed into practical technologies, and those technologies being combined through engineering into complex devices delivering new functionalities – that's true innovation. And in the world of business, that means new products, delivering profitable new sales, growing your business and staying ahead of the competition.

Yet because of the overuse of "innovation" as a term in the business world today, even I'm embarrassed to say, in the marketing literature for my own business (TTIP Consulting), I am always a little uncomfortable using the word "innovation" because of the diluted ambiguity that hangs around it in the business world today. But that's what we do at TTIP Consulting, that's the sector we work in. So until I can think of a better word, I'm going to stick with it. Maybe I'm just as guilty of jumping on the bandwagon, running an "innovation" consulting company and writing a book with "innovation" in the title? Who knows? Though in my defence, I have been doing this for over 30 years! It's in my blood, it's what I do and it's what I know.

And while I'm on a roll about how terms have become distorted in today's business world, even the word "technology" has been hijacked these days. As we have just established, technology is the practical application of science, so that means new engineering designs, new materials, new devices, new systems, everything with a basis in science to make it work, that creates new functionality. So when did "technology" get to mean software, or get to mean IT? When you look at many so-called "technology" conferences and books, they are actually focused purely on the IT sector. I know things like fintech, medtech, cloud computing and cybersecurity are all massive industries now, and that the IT sector is the biggest growth industry of the last twenty years, but when did IT become to only denote "technology"? Technology has also grown within the world of executive search and management consulting to just mean IT. When you say to people in the business world that you work in technology, often they think you are talking about IT, and they seem to think you work in the software/IT industry. This is just pure laziness (and a degree of ignorance). IT is not technology, it is just a subclass of "technology", it is a specific area of the practical application of science, that is built on the science of semiconducting materials, combined with electrical engineering to create devices and systems that can be controlled by writing code. So please, let's not simplify IT as being "technology". It is, and has always been, "information technology".

But why has IT become so dominant in business? Simple, because as the biggest growth sector of the last two decades, there are many people making a lot of money out of it. And this is translated into a perception that IT and digitalisation are now the most important things today, that in some way it stands apart and alone from the rest of industry, that all this data that the software handles is out there hanging around somewhere in the IT ether. And using words like "the cloud" just adds to the perception, but of course the reality is that it isn't floating around out there in some mysterious electronic ether. All the data and all the code sit on physical servers, designed by engineers, built by manufacturers, using cutting edge, highly advanced materials developed by incredibly clever and talented technical people. Software, of course, only works if it has hardware to work on. It does not and cannot exist on its own. The IT industry serves the needs of the rest of the existing industries, of manufacturing, of finance, of healthcare, of society in general. A great, unstoppable advance in digitalisation everywhere these days. But it isn't really replacing anything – it's all additive. IT can and does certainly make things more efficient, but we still need the hardware to run the code, we still need engineers to design the hardware, we still need production engineers to make the hardware a reality, and we still need an industrial manufacturing economy to produce the stuff. So the whole of the IT industry feeds off the real world, it doesn't replace it. So how has it become so dominant? It really is just an illusion fuelled by marketing and the propagation of the IT industry across social media platforms.

So in this book, I hope I have made myself crystal clear, when I talk about "innovation", I mean new product development that adds new revenue streams and delivers real, profitable business growth, and when I talk about "technology", I mean the practical application of science, in all is numerous forms.

Now, I've got that off my chest, we can begin.

Andy

1

INNOVATION MATTERS, SO WHY DO BUSINESSES STRUGGLE WITH IT?

> There is a huge gap between what works in the laboratory and what it takes to commercialise.
>
> Mike Murray, Chief Technology Officer at The Vita Group

Innovation has been my life. I spent 30 years in industry developing new products, using technology to create competitive advantage and help customers improve their businesses. And if you're one of those hundreds of thousands of people across the world involved in creating new technologies and delivering innovation, have no illusion: what we do matters.

I have been lucky enough to enjoy a varied career over the years. I have been involved in developing, designing or leading the development of numerous advanced material and industrial engineering solutions that delivered improved functionality and solved real, practical problems across a wide variety of industries including oil and gas, automotive, aerospace, iron and steel, aluminium, foundry, refractories, fire protection, power generation, energy and renewables, semiconductor and medical devices.

At times in my career I have been privileged to work on some extraordinary things. I have worked on really cutting edge, ultra-high purity chemical vapour deposition material solutions for billion-dollar semiconductor fabs. At other times, I have worked on life-changing medical device technologies, like ceramic hip joints, neuro-stimulation devices and cochlear implants. This last one is technology that helps deaf people hear again! How life-changing is that? Watching the videos of device trials and seeing the first time a deaf child hears its mother's voice is one of the most heart-tugging moments I have ever felt in my career. I'm welling up now just writing about it. This stuff matters. Innovation matters. And when you're sitting in the plush corporate headquarters of global giants like Intel preparing for a meeting, or sitting in Houston at the headquarters of one of the mega global oil corporations, it certainly feels good, it certainly feels like your career is on the right path, it certainly feels like what you're doing matters.

But it wasn't always like that. I started my career in far less sexy technology. I started out in refractories, developing refractory castable products (essentially, these are concretes for use at very high temperatures and in extreme corrosion environments). This is real formulation technology, working with ultra-complex mixtures of natural and synthetic materials and chemical additives – very complicated science. But when you're a technologist in a laboratory mixing one grey powder with another grey powder, and casting hundreds of dull, grey three-inch cube samples, and doing endless physical testing and endless environmental testing on those cubes, life doesn't feel so sexy. It doesn't feel like innovation matters. Life feels rather dull and grey, like those test samples, and it's hard to get excited that what you are doing really matters. Developing technology and remaining motivated can be a hard slog for those in the laboratory.

But what I have come to understand over the years, with the wisdom that only age and developing perspective seems to deliver, is that even in this area of technology, what you are doing really matters. Even though maybe I didn't appreciate it at the time, the "dull grey powder" work I was doing really was making a difference. If you're working in refractory castables, maybe, as was my case, the product you are developing is a new formulation that will allow customers in the petrochemical industry to line a new reaction vessel, running at much higher process temperatures, allowing them to significantly improve their process efficiencies, improving their yields and reducing their process times, and saving the industry billions of dollars in energy costs a year. How impressive is that? Such an innovation would make much more efficient use of the world's resources. (I used this same example in my first book to illustrate the innovation barrier "dumbing down your products" [see the discussion of *Transforming Technology into Profit* in Chapter 2]).

Maybe instead of refractory applications, your "grey powder" lab work is aimed at developing a new ultra-high strength civil concrete formulation, one that would allow civil engineers to design and build taller and longer bridges, spanning previously untraversable valleys, joining hitherto poorly linked regions of a country. Such a material and such a capability could deliver a huge increase in trade and would result in significantly developing the local economies. Think of the billions of dollars of trade that could bring into a region. This would make a real difference to the quality of peoples' lives and to the lives of their communities. Innovation matters, no matter what you are working on.

Innovation always makes a difference to peoples' lives, either directly (like new medical technologies) or indirectly (like making better use of the world's resources). Yet in the world of innovation, everyone always focuses on science and technology. They focus on the nuts and bolts of what it is and how it works. Industry conferences are littered with presentations of clever new products as part of marketing efforts, but they are largely focused on what it is and how it works. Why? Because it's interesting, because it's new, because it's clever, because it's cutting edge and because it's sexy. And so people often don't see beyond that. But what people often fail to focus on and fail to talk about, is what these technologies actually do, what new functionalities they deliver. This is what makes the difference to people and society, not *what it is*, but *what it does*. So whatever area of science and technology you find yourself working in, to maintain motivation, remember to focus on what it does, not what it is. What you are doing will genuinely impact the quality of people's lives one way or another, either directly or indirectly. This stuff matters. Innovation matters.

Is the Innovation Industry Really Working?

So, if innovation is so important, and if innovation matters so much, then why are so many businesses so bad at it? Why do so many businesses struggle to grow through innovation and new products? A 2016 Bain and Company study concluded that a massive 89% of businesses struggle to grow, struggle to consistently deliver sustainable increase in profit and revenue. Yes, that does read 89%. This highlights just how difficult it is for businesses to grow. And if you are working in a business that is one of those 89% struggling to grow, then maybe you can take some comfort in the fact that you are not alone, not by a long way. And it's not that these businesses are all run by incompetents. Most businesses are run by well-educated, experienced, professional, highly capable and highly driven individuals, many with MBAs and other high-level business management qualifications. So why is it that so many businesses struggle to grow?

When digging into the underlying causes of why the figure is so high, the Bain and Company study discovered that 85% of the executives they surveyed, and a full 94% of senior executives running companies with over $5 billion in revenue, considered "internal factors" as key impediments to profitable growth. And it is exactly those "internal factors" that we will be exploring in this book. What they are, how to identify them and what you can do about them. In this book, I will show that it is possible to analyse your own business, highlight what "internal factors" are holding your business back from growth and how to unblock them. This book is all about giving a name to those internal factors and taking a methodical, and proven, approach to dealing with them, so that you can unlock the true potential of your own business to grow by adding new revenue streams and new, saleable, profitable products. And it is my experience that these "internal factors" run right across most businesses, regardless of size, scale and complexity. I have seen these same challenges holding back companies turning over millions of dollars, tens of millions of dollars and hundreds of millions of dollars throughout my career, not just the mega-corporations.

And it's not just the Bain and Company report that highlights and attempts to quantify today's innovation growth dilemma. McKinsey, Boston Consulting Group, PwC and almost every other leading management consultancy firm have all done their own research and published their own reports on the subject. Whilst the absolute numbers might differ, the conclusions are always the same. All such reports conclude that the vast majority of senior executives agree that innovation is one of the key drivers for growth in their businesses, but in contrast to this, the vast majority of the same executives are also generally disappointed with their own innovation programmes and recognise that they have been largely unsuccessful or at least underwhelming. For example, the analysis reported by McKinsey found that 84% of executives agreed that innovation is important to the growth strategy of their business, but it also found that only 6% of them are satisfied with the innovation performance of their business, with very few of them claiming to know exactly what the problem is and how to improve their innovation and R&D capabilities.

But how can this be? There is so much published on all aspects of business innovation. There are hundreds of new books dealing with some aspect or other of innovation published each year, if you trawl through Amazon and Google. There are professors of innovation at all major business schools and universities these days. There are an ever-increasing number of innovation conferences and seminars taking place every week across the world. There are endless blog articles published daily from "experts" right across the internet, not to mention the innovation analysis reports from the big management consultancy firms I mentioned earlier. And you can even study to get qualifications in various aspects of innovation, both at business schools and through online learning. There is so much "expertise" on the subject, and much of it has been around for decades. So given that there are thousands of "experts" out there offering their services to help companies with their innovation programmes, tens of thousands of reference materials to study, and hundreds of forums to discuss ideas and get advice from, and have been for many, many years, why is it that today, 89% of businesses still continue to struggle to grow? And why do the vast majority of the executives running them openly admit that they have no clue how to improve the innovation performance of their business? There seems to be a very fundamental and serious issue with the innovation industry.

You could possibly argue that the innovation industry has so far only been able to focus on and support the 11% of businesses that are reportedly growing, but this seems very unlikely given the breadth and extent of the innovation industry these days, and the high profile company logos that almost every innovation consultancy displays on their website as their pool of customers they have helped. And of course, there are successes, surely someone would have noticed well before now if all these innovation support businesses weren't delivering anything positive. But for 89% of businesses still to be struggling to grow, any such successes must be isolated. And the most telling thing to recognise of all is that those big global management consultancy firms that are reporting that 89% of businesses are struggling to grow (given that the Top Ten hoover up 56% of the global management consultancy market) are the very same consultancy firms that have been trying to help most of those companies grow; this suggests heavily that what they, and others in this industry, are doing is not working effectively. This is the scandal permeating through the whole of the innovation industry today, and this is why I opened this section with the title "Is the Innovation Industry Really Working?" But more on this later.

Despite all the advice and guidance from innovation consultancies, the reality that many businesses eventually discover, after pouring huge resources into innovation programmes, is that innovation is not easy, it is not simple and that there is no one-size-fits-all solution. Creating a new role with "innovation" in the title is rarely the answer. Launching a grand, new "innovation" programme is rarely the answer. These things can be a start, but the start of a long and difficult business transformation process that in reality needs to be fluid and managed through experience, not by following the "innovation-by-numbers" formula that too many "experts" follow. This is why identifying the "internal factors" that are holding back your business from innovation and from growth needs to be the first step. And those "internal factors" will be unique to your business, because every business is different.

You can read as many case studies as you want about how other companies have attempted to grow through innovation, but do not make the mistake of thinking that just because it worked at ABC Ltd, it's going to work at your company. Every company is different: different products, different technology, different markets served and different channels to market, but above all, the biggest differentiator is the different people. People are everything in business. The way people interact and behave is a product of their personalities, the organisational structure within which they have to act and the way they are managed and rewarded. All of these things add up to a completely unique environment that exists within your business, and a completely unique culture. People are ultimately the reason why there cannot, and can never be, a one-size-fits-all solution to innovation, and why innovation programmes are extremely difficult to make a success of. And if you don't start from that premise, you are very unlikely to succeed in growing your business through innovation and through differentiated new products.

Think back to all those industry conferences we mentioned earlier, to all the exciting and interesting new technologies and products they showcase: how many of those new products are actually commercially successful? How many are delivering, or are going to deliver, the profits that the business invested so heavily in to achieve? Just because the company's innovation efforts resulted in something new, doesn't mean that there is a real market need for it, doesn't mean that it has the full buy-in of the top management to support it, and doesn't mean that it is actually delivering sales. Announcing a new product is just another stepping stone on the long road to commercial success. To get to that point, they have surely had to deal with a whole bunch of "internal factors", but their journey is by no means over.

The Innovation Process

To start to understand what these "internal factors" are and how they hold back business growth, we first need a quick reminder of how innovation works in a business. We need to remind ourselves of the "process of innovation". My previous book, *Transforming Technology into Profit*, was largely built around this process, and used the well-recognised steps of the process to form the structure of the book, around which I could weave a narrative to explain some practical approaches for effective management of each step and to highlight many of the barriers that can and do create problems in trying to manage the process and deliver new products. The full set of steps that make up the "process of innovation" are summarised in the diagram below, along with the business systems used to manage each step. If you need more detail on any of the steps, or any specific terms or phrases used, please refer back to my previous book.

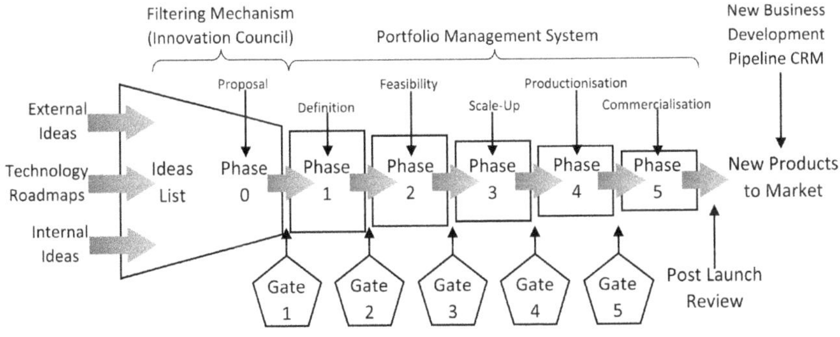

The process of innovation is well represented by the classic innovation funnel model, and is made up of the following key steps:

1) Idea generation – this is the first phase of the process of creating new products, which involves collating a long list of ideas for new products and services to diversify and grow your business. These can incorporate enhancements to existing products or completely new products in your existing markets, or step change products in new markets, depending on the ambition you have set for your business in your strategy. Ideas can be pulled from multiple sources, both internally (including internal sales reports, new business project and portfolio reviews, technology roadmaps, brainstorming events) and externally (including technology scanning, intellectual property scanning, market intelligence, trade shows/exhibitions, industry working groups, competitive analysis/intelligence, direct customer contacts, voice of customer exercises).
2) Idea selection – once you have built your long list of potential ideas, you then have to rank them in some kind of order that is relevant to your business and the markets you serve, such that you can create a priority list of which ideas are the most likely to deliver the growth you are looking for. Typical criteria employed for ranking ideas are as follows:
    a. Strategic Assessment Criteria (e.g. strategic fit, ethics and EHS, new or me too, market need, potential annual sales value).
    b. Technical Assessment Criteria (e.g. technical capability, technology protectability, technology disruption level).
    c. Resource Assessment Criteria (e.g. estimated project cost, estimated timescale to complete, estimated investment cost, access to market).

    Which criteria you choose for ranking and prioritisation will be influenced by the scale of ambition of your business strategy. The idea list for a business that aims to grow sales incrementally by 5% a year versus one that aims to double their sales every year for five years is likely to look very different, and the appetite for risk in each business will need to be correspondingly different.

    Once you have your list of potential ideas in priority order, you can then make a decision about which of the top ranked ideas you are going to take forward as potential projects. Where are you going to draw the line? Top five, top ten, top 50? This will depend on how deep your company pockets are and the growth targets you need to fulfil. These top projects then get resources and individuals assigned to them to expand the idea, explore the product concepts and market landscape in more detail, and prepare a formal business case in the form of a project proposal. This is often considered to be the first part of the phase-gate project management process, usually formally called "phase 0". All the proposals will be assessed by a representative senior team, called the "innovation council" in some businesses, who will make the final decision on which project proposals should be funded and become formal projects to enter the company's project management system.

3) Project implementation – the phase-gate system is the most common style of project management system employed by industrial companies to manage new business and new product development projects, also called the "waterfall model" in the software industry. There are alternative approaches to project management available, including Agile, some of which will be explored later in this book. The phase-gate approach has proven successful in many businesses in this context because it overlays a rigorous, methodical approach to managing the progress of projects, through a series of carefully documented phases, coupled with formalised decision gate checklists. The particular value of the checklists is that they enable teams to ask the "right" questions, ones that the organisation has identified over the many years it has been commercialising new products. Whichever process you run with, it is only as good as the skill, experience and discipline of the individual(s) managing it. There are several different ways of describing the different phases, but the ones I have found work best are as follows:
    a. Phase 1: project definition – this is where the original project proposal that got the idea through to a formally funded project gets a much more rigorous treatment, transforming an outline business proposal into a fully documented project plan with timescales and milestones, a detailed project scope, and clearly defined technical targets. Phase 1 is usually about exploring the technology platform underpinning the new product, so will

likely require some degree of practical early concept development work in the laboratory, and certainly will involve visiting customers to understand the target application firsthand.

b. Phase 2: project feasibility – this is where the technology platform built in Phase 1 gets refined into a more practical and exploitable form, and so this is where the bulk of the R&D work gets done in a project, working through proof of concept and leading to prototyping, either still at the lab scale or on a pilot line. It is important to continuously connect with end users during this phase to ensure that what you are developing does not drift away from something that customers actually want to buy.
c. Phase 3: scale-up – this is where the first small-scale production runs of the prototypes are made, either on a pilot line or moving from pilot to pre-production, producing small volumes on a full-scale production line, depending on the nature of the technology/product. Scale-up is often the most challenging and time-consuming phase of all, because the work always unearths things you did not anticipate about the technology you have developed, requiring significant process engineering to deal with any issues.
d. Phase 4: productionisation – this is where the production prototype truly becomes a product that can be manufactured at scale, repeatably and reliably. Product specifications are finalised, standard operating procedures (SOPs) are written and a quality control plan is set. A full-scale programme of customer trials will be ongoing during this phase.
e. Phase 5: commercialisation – this is where your new product truly hits the market. You may already have had some early sales through large-scale customer trials in earlier phases, but phase 5 is when everything is ready for the official launch. Marketing literature will be prepared, the sales campaign and business plan will be established, and a launch event organised. This phase is usually considered complete when the sales plan has been worked through, at which point, the project is effectively also considered complete. Launching and building sales takes time but is influenced heavily by how passionately the business

believes in the new product. Once the sales plan is completed, maybe one year after launch, it is useful to have a post-implementation (or post-launch) review to dissect how successful the project has been, and to pick up and act on any learning points.

4) Portfolio management – as your business will most likely be juggling multiple new business and new product development projects at the same time, another key aspect of the innovation process is the system for managing the whole portfolio of projects. The level of complexity and sophistication of the system will depend on the scale and diversity of your business, with the most comprehensive of systems documenting the following criteria:
    a. Project identification (e.g. project owner, lead business, currency, project ID code, project start date, project completion date, project timescale).
    b. Project details (e.g. project type, product description, product group, application description).
    c. Customer and market details (e.g. new or existing customer, target customer name, customer number, customer type, origin of lead, market, competitor).
    d. Project status (e.g. current project phase, an indication of whether the project is on track, e.g. red/yellow/green "traffic light" indicator, probability of success, date of last data entry).
    e. Financial details (e.g. total annual sales potential, sales forecast by quarter, total estimated customer spend, total "through" % gross margin, capex required (value), capex required (date).

   Keeping an eye of the status of all the projects in your portfolio with respect to the inevitably changing priorities in any business is essential to help target your finite resources and bring the most lucrative projects to market as quickly as possible.

Innovation Needs a Lot of Ideas – There Are No Eureka Moments

We concluded in the introduction to this book that, whichever way you choose to dress it up with confusing management speak and buzzwords, new product and new business development innovation is a fundamental set of skills and processes that every single business needs in order to maintain and increase profitability. And earlier in this chapter, we made reference to the many recent business analysis reports that all conclude that the vast majority of businesses are just not good at it. But why is this? Why are most businesses lousy at growing through new products? One reason is that those businesses almost certainly have no process to generate and capture ideas, and innovation needs a lot of ideas to thrive. They may have good people with good ideas, but if they have no mechanism to capture and process them, then they are not going to see the light of day. And most businesses also grossly underestimate the number of new ideas they are going to have to work with to create a new product.

I mentioned – in my first book on innovation, *Transforming Technology into Profit* – the 1997 study by Stevens and Burley, "3,000 Raw Ideas = 1 Commercial Success!", published in *Research Technology Magazine*, which concluded that "across most industries, it appears to require 3,000 raw ideas to produce one substantially new, commercially successful industrial product". 3,000 to 1, that's quite shockingly inefficient when you first see it. But if you've been involved in business for a number of years, you can start to appreciate that this 3,000:1 seems to match pretty realistically what actually happens in a business.

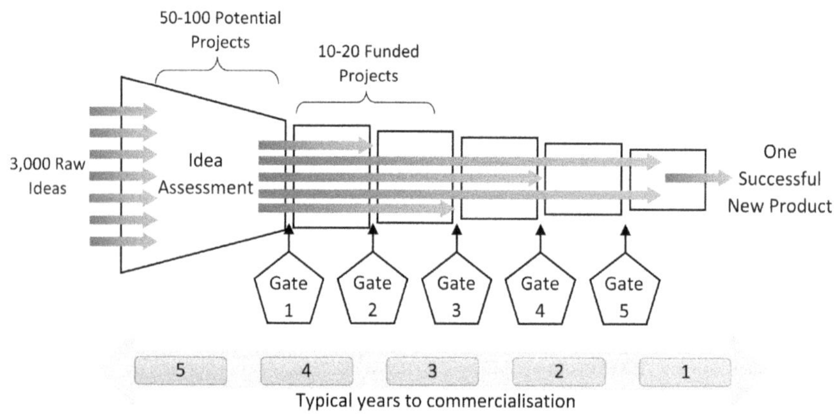

Mapping the 3,000:1 against the "process of innovation" steps, sifting through 3,000 ideas might typically throw up 50 to 100 ideas that might make suitable projects with the potential to deliver a positive contribution to the business. And assessing 50 to 100 potential projects might typically lead to 10 to 20 funded projects, depending on how deep the business' pockets are for new product and new business development projects. And once these 10 to 20 projects are actually worked on, we know from running a phase-gate type process that not all of these projects will make it to commercialisation. Some will be killed along the way at one or another of the phase-gate meetings and others will be shelved. So, of ten+ projects, maybe two of them will make it to commercialisation. That means of 3,000 raw ideas, maybe two will become new products that make it to market.

There are also plenty of studies that have looked at the success rates of new product introductions. Many published articles and books refer to such studies, though each citation seems to distort the message a little each time as it gets further and further away from the source. One frequently referenced, and quite scary, quote from the late Clayton Christensen (Harvard Business School), whose sad death was announced just as we went into the editing phase of this book, states that "each year more than 30,000 new consumer products are launched and 95% of them fail". But another version of the same "quote" states it's 80% (Schroeder 2017). Another quote from Inez Blackburn (University of Toronto), suggests that the failure rate for new products launched in the grocery sector is 70–80%. If these are true, and they are all scary prospects after the millions of dollars your company might have spent in taking an idea all the way through to commercialisation, they highlight the risk-taking element of any new product development activity your business attempts, and also serve to question the effectiveness of all the well-constructed and professionally managed innovation processes in place at businesses around the world. If all they can deliver is a 10–30% success rate, then we really should be questioning the effectiveness of all these processes and the people that manage them.

But it takes more than just new product introductions to keep a business afloat and much more to make it grow sustainably, because you also have to consider what's happening with all the standard products, which by definition, will still represent the vast majority of a company's sales up to and at the point of any new product introduction. Considering the natural degree of market and customer churn that any standard business has to deal with every year, and the manufacturing costs versus profitability pressures that these standard product lines are continuously under, and the constant competitive pressures that the standard product portfolio will be enduring, then the new product launch has to be pretty spectacularly successful to counteract all of these things that are going on in the business at the same time, and raise the company up to the growth levels it hopes to achieve.

However, deeper investigation of such oft-quoted statements about the success of new product introductions suggests that this 70–90% failure rate is actually an "urban myth", and that literature (and even the people who are claimed to have made these statements) does not support such numbers. George Castellion and Stephen K. Markham's article "New Product Failure Rates: Influence of Argumentum ad Populum and Self-Interest" (2013) digs deep into this urban legend. Part of the confusion is down to how you measure failure rate, with some studies really talking about ideas of successful products, rather than the success of actual launched products. In terms of the failure rate of new products actually launched on to the market, their study concludes it is around 40%. Logic would say that the actual figure is going to depend on market sector, and their study reports failure rates averaging 40%, plus or minus 5% depending on sector. The earlier Stevens and Burley study suggests that the failure rates are around 60%.

Trying to agree what the real number for percentage of new product failures is always going to be an academic exercise. What really matters to any business is what successes you are actually having with your new product introductions. Sure, having an industry benchmark can be somewhat helpful in understanding how good or bad your company is at this, but ultimately any company needs to measure itself, set targets and work to improve. So, sifting through all the urban myth nonsense and the more rigorous studies concluding 40 or 60%, I am perfectly happy to consider that new product failure rates are around 50% plus or minus 10%. This means, going back to the earlier raw ideas model, of the two products that made it to market from the original 3,000 ideas, then only one is likely to be a commercial success. So the 3,000:1 starts to feel real. And again, for those of us who have worked for many years in business, we all know that the timescale from idea to commercial success can be many, many years, easily five or more. Just think how many resources, how much time and effort is required by a business to generate all those ideas, assess them, prioritise them, staff and resource the ensuing development projects, scale up and productionise the new technologies, conduct customer trials and set the sales and marketing resource loose to commercialise the new products. All over many years, and all of it delivering zero return until one of the new products becomes a success and starts to repay the investment.

Innovation Competes with Other Investment Options

When you truly start to look at the whole innovation process holistically, it is quite scary the amount of time and resources a business needs to commit to drive its growth for the future. And this is one of the challenges with resourcing innovation in a business, because there are other options that a business can choose to achieve growth, other ways it can invest, all of which are competing for the same pot of money. This is another of the reasons that businesses struggle with innovation, because investment is usually spread across several different areas, leading to unfocused and diluted initiatives with innovation competing internally for funds with all the other forms of investment. Now, a business is unlikely to lay all of its bets across all possible investment options. You wouldn't place your bets on every number, every combination, on both red and black on a roulette table all at the same time, would you? Which investment areas a business chooses to fund depends on their business strategy, assuming they have one (see *Transforming Technology into Profit*, Chapter 2). And let's be clear, the investments that your business are making are absolutely bets. You have no way of predicting with certainty which of those bets is going to deliver the huge return you are planning for. Of course, business is all about assessing the risks, doing your homework, doing your due diligence, looking at the investment situation from multiple angles and from multiple expert points of view, all so that you can minimise the risk to your cash and to your business. But the real-world roulette table of business that you are playing on is a highly complex VUCA environment (volatile, uncertain, complex and ambiguous), that however much data capture and analysis you throw at, still has high levels of volatility, uncertainty, complexity and ambiguity, so your investment is still a bet.

So what are these competing options that a business can consider to invest in for growth? The diagram below summarises the main types. The investment options fall broadly into two main types, referred to as "organic", which are all options designed to grow your existing business based on what you have inside the business today, and "inorganic", which are all options designed to grow your business by adding new things that currently don't exist within the business. Note that we are not considering here all the myriad ways that a business invests in itself on a day-to-day basis, like continuous improvement in business and production processes to reduce costs, marketing activities to grow sales, staff training to improve efficiencies, etc. Yes, they all cost money, but I see those as all the day-to-day stuff of running a modern business. What we are considering here are those large sums of cash that a business has to lay down to fund their big ambitious growth initiatives. These are the large bets that a business is placing for its future, and the ones that are competing with investment in innovation.

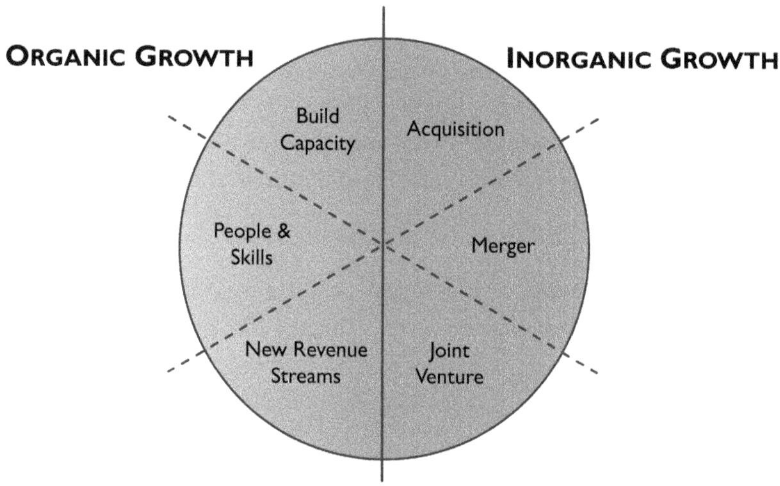

Investment Options

Organic Growth

1) Build production capacity – if your business is doing well, gaining new customers, growing its sales and capturing new markets and geographies, then at some point, your growth will become constrained by your company's ability to manufacture and deliver its goods and/or services. This is true whether your business makes physical products or provides services. As your business grows, hopefully you see this bottleneck to your future growth coming down the line, so you can prepare. And you will need to prepare, because building production capacity takes time and money. Maybe it just requires you to add a new manufacturing cell within your existing premises, maybe it requires you to build an extension to your factory and set up new production facilities in there, maybe it requires you to build a new

factory in a new location. Each of these requires increasing amounts of investment and increasing timescales to plan, execute and bring online. And whether you are in the business of manufacturing physical items or not, building production capacity always requires adding and training people, which adds to the cost and timescale that needs to be factored into the project.

Whatever scale you are working on, physically building production capacity is a capital investment project, because you are adding physical assets to a company's balance sheet. During my long career in industry, I have been involved in building several factories, including both greenfield (i.e. land that has never previously been built on) and brownfield (i.e. land that has already been built on) projects, and in relocating and re-engineering numerous manufacturing lines across the world. I have led the construction of new factories in China, I have moved whole factories out of North America and Europe to new locations and I have transferred numerous production processes across Europe and out to Asia and South America. And what I have learnt, is that to be successful, each of these types of investment should be treated as a major project, with a project manager assigned, a budget allocated, rigorous project management systems put in place and communication and accountability up to the board of directors. Otherwise, things will drift, timescales will be missed, budgets will overrun. In particular, the bigger the capital project, the more you need to consider assigning a dedicated project manager who does nothing else but manage that project. It is very tempting to use your existing management team and just assign capital projects as extra jobs to people, but that is just diluting their time, when they presumably already have a day job, adding a whole lot of risk to project delivery.

2) Investing in people and skills – another constraint you will hit as your business grows is people and skills. Just like production capacity, the number of employees and the range and level of skills within the business will limit what you can do in terms of servicing clients. At some point as your business grows, everyone in the business will become fully occupied and you will start to have to turn customers away or risk disappointing them with very long delivery times. Another consequence of growth is that at some point, the business

will inevitably reach a critical mass for which you need to add another layer of management. You know when you have reached this point, because you cannot physically talk to everyone on a day-to-day basis, you will not be able to retain everyone's name, or be aware of what's going on everywhere. It depends on the type of business, and how it is organised, but typically, critical mass is achieved around 50–70 people. When your business has grown this big, you will inevitably have to let go of direct control of the day-to day-aspects of a business: uncomfortable for many entrepreneurs, but unavoidable if you want your business to continue to grow.

As part of investing for future growth, as you monitor business growth and better understand your market sectors and dynamics, you can begin to anticipate and prepare for this critical mass and manage your way through it by a phased campaign of hiring and training staff. This may require a change in premises for the business as well in order to cope with the expansion of people. This kind of growth investment can go hand in hand with building production capacity, though usually there is an offset in timing. It really depends on the nature of your business, your channels to market and your business strategy.

As an alternative to investing purely in employee numbers to deliver growth, a business may instead need to develop or add in new skills to extend or improve a company's offerings. This will usually take the form of an extensive training programme, targeted at the relevant department, e.g. improving sales team effectiveness. And almost inevitably, such training will be delivered by an external consulting company. Such targeted training programmes for skills enhancement can be expensive and time-consuming activities. In large multinationals, these can be global programmes run over several years, making them seriously big investments. Monitoring the value of such investments can be challenging, depending on how directly the skills they are embedding in the company contribute to the bottom line.

3) Develop new revenue streams – in any market, there is only so much a business can grow before it reaches a natural limit, before it maximises its market share. Where this limit is will depend on the size and complexity of the market, the number and quality of competitors and exactly where and how your own business plays within the various

market segments. Building production capacity and investing in people and skills will all help get you to this growth limit. Once you max out on market share, then there is only one way to grow from that position organically, and that is to add new revenue streams. This is where you will need to invest in developing new products and services, or in improving your existing product line sufficiently so that it taps into a new market or segment. This is the growth investment option where innovation and new product development come into play. But you cannot wait until you reach your market share limit to start investing in innovation, because we have already established that it takes time to get from seed ideas to real, commercialised products – often many years. So this is why a business needs to be investing in innovation almost continuously, in parallel to managing its production capacity, headcount and people skills, because they serve different purposes along a company's growth trajectory.

All businesses start with innovation, they start with an idea or a prototype that captures the imagination of consumers and of investors, and they then grow from this original innovation, building their business around this product or group of products. That growth needs continuous investment in production capacity, headcount and people skills to feed demand, but if there is no further investment in product innovation from the initial launch, then that company is inevitably limiting its ability to grow, it is automatically setting a ceiling to the market share that it can possibly achieve organically. Now that ceiling might not be reached for many years, and the profit that can be generated along the way may be considerable, all dependent on the nature of the business and the size and competitive landscape of the market segment it plays in, but reach it one day you will. Innovation is what allows a business to push beyond this barrier, which is why it is a fundamental skill that all businesses need to get better at. The Bain and Company study mentioned earlier in this chapter does attempt to list some of the "internal factors" that executives believe are constraining growth in 89% of businesses, and comparing these various soundbites against my own 30-year experience in industry, what I see as the real, underlying reason that 89% of businesses are struggling to grow is because they have reached their natural growth ceiling and are now struggling with the next step along the business maturity timeline, that of innovation. Consequently, they are finding it very difficult to successfully add new and profitable revenue streams to push beyond their market share limit. These are the elusive "internal factors" executives refer to in the study. How you go about adding new revenue streams, how you identify and target opportunities, how you transform these into product development projects and how you manage these projects through productionisation and on to successful commercialisation is largely the subject of my previous book, *Transforming Technology into Profit*, so I refer you to that book to better understand the mechanics of the process.

Inorganic Growth

1) Acquisition – a practical alternative to any of the above organic growth investment options, be it expanding production capacity, adding people and skills or developing new products to add new revenue streams, is simply to go out and purchase a company that already has the relevant production capacity, or the relevant people and skills or has new products that would automatically add new revenue streams to your business. With an acquisition, you will almost certainly be buying an existing customer base, so you can increase your market share overnight, and/or add new market segments to your portfolio. Sounds simple, and potentially quicker than having to build or develop all this stuff yourself, so why bother to do all this organically? An acquisition involves one legal entity taking over another, and the reality of managing an effective takeover of another business, and integration of one business into another, is not to be taken lightly. It absorbs a huge amount of management time and energy, which may be better spent on organic growth activities, as they are potentially more under your control.
2) Merger – a merger is similar to an acquisition in that two companies join together, but with a merger, two separate legal entities combine to create a new, joint organisation, which becomes a new legal entity. With an acquisition, the company that acquires the other retains its original legal status. Mergers are generally less common than acquisitions, but can occur when bringing the two companies together

offers additional growth potential from combining complementary technologies, products, market access, production capacities and/or locations.

3) Joint Venture – a joint venture (JV) is a new business created by two or more separate businesses, so unlike acquisitions or mergers, both starting entities remain and continue to trade separately. The JV becomes a third, stand-alone business. The reasons for creating a JV are similar to those of a merger: potential benefits from combining skills, technologies, market access, etc., but without the huge upheaval, and risk to the businesses of fully integrating the two companies. This is not to suggest that creating and managing a JV is easier. A JV has its own management needs and business risks. One common style of JV is when a Western company wants to set up in China. Partnering with a Chinese company allows immediate access to the local market. During my career, when I lived in China, I was involved in setting up a number of new JV businesses, both in China and throughout the Asian region, so I have experienced firsthand the challenges of setting up and managing joint ventures, particularly those associated with a Western company partnering with a company on the other side of the planet. What all those experiences taught me, was that going into a JV is not to be taken lightly, as it takes a lot of hard work. It is like a marriage. It needs constant relationship building and you cannot become complacent. Finding the right partner is critical at the start, and having shared alignment on goals for the business, and shared ethics and business approach are very important to give a JV every chance of success. And just like a marriage, what your partner wants at the start of the relationship can change over time. What might be a successful partnership at first can easily drift over the years. Just like a marriage, JV partners can find themselves drifting apart, leading to more arguments and bad feelings. JVs need to be worked on and not taken for granted.

Getting the balance right between all these different types of growth investment is a challenge for any business. There are advantages and disadvantages to both routes, and your business strategy is the ultimate guide to helping you decide which investments are the best ones for your business.

Advantages and Disadvantages

Organic Growth

1) Advantages – the biggest advantage of going down any of the organic investment routes to fund growth is that it is all within your own control. Whether you are choosing to invest in new production capacity, hiring and training people or trying to create new products to diversify your portfolio, these are all things which are doable within the confines of your own, existing business, that fit largely within your existing organisational structure and that mostly utilise your existing business processes. For any mature business, it's unlikely it's the first time you have built a new manufacturing line, or hired new people, or developed a new product, so you will already have some competence and some internal resources and expertise to handle these, all of which reduces the risk to your investment. Sure, the bigger and bolder the investment plan you are implementing, the more likely you will be stepping beyond your existing skills and capacity, and that you will need to hire some new skills, either as new positions within your company, or temporary roles just to implement the project. But still, you are working off a base of existing competence and presumably some track record of success. And so the whole investment process will be being managed by people who understand your business strategy, have a good network of internal connections around the company, who likely already work together as a team, and already know well the working culture and how to get things done – all of which are real advantages in trying to make any investment successful and in delivering it as quickly as possible. There will be less unknowns to consider and fewer curveballs coming your way, all minimising the risk to the investment. There will also be fewer restructuring and integration challenges to manage through, as you will likely be adding people into existing teams, using existing HR procedures, or creating a new team, rather than having to handle the painful headcount reduction exercises that can result from some of the inorganic investment options. Overall, organic investment gives the business more control over where the business is headed, and the rate at which it heads there, leading to more sustainable growth. Organic growth is also important if you want to attract interest from

investors, because it signals a healthy, well-managed business, and a safe bet to deliver good returns.

2) Disadvantages – one of the big disadvantages of going down any of the organic investment routes is that it is generally the slowest way to achieve growth. Depending on the complexity and scale of your operations, to build a new production line may require up to two years from the initial decision point before it is on stream and delivering products to your customers, and if your plan is to build a whole new factory, it can take two to five years to get to this stage. Similarly, finding, hiring, integrating and training new staff is a very lengthy process. And as we have already explored earlier in this book, that new product development can easily take five years or more to start paying back the investment. In addition to this, as you will be managing any investment plan with your existing resources – at least to begin with – this automatically puts a limit on the scale and boldness of investment you can handle as a business. Unless you have a senior role whose job is to manage special projects, with a dedicated team, then everyone you will be using to implement any of your organic investment projects already has a full-time job, and so the growth projects can easily become a distraction from, or be prioritised below, the running of the day-to-day business. And it's the same with funding, which has to come from your current reserves, additional business loans or other forms of outside investment – all of which have to keep pace with the needs of your growth plans as they arise (there's a great case study on how this can go badly wrong in Chapter 5 of this book). All of these manpower and funding constraints naturally suppress the pace at which organic growth can be rolled out. But it is not only internal factors which can hold back organic growth efforts, external factors too play a significant role. For capacity and people investment, the very market you play in will present a natural constraint. There is only so much market growth you can grab, determined by the boundaries of your business strategy in terms of geographic markets served and by the industry sector within which you are active. You can aim to increase market share, but the annual growth rate of your market segment will also present a major constraint to your growth potential, as will the activities of your competitors, who can seriously impact your growth plans as you roll them

out, and you are particularly vulnerable to this given the long execution timescales involved. The degree of "mergers and acquisitions" activity in your market sector can also impact your own growth plans, as the amalgamation of key competitors can quickly see you outmanoeuvred in the market place, through new pricing models and supply channels. This is why focusing on growth through new products is so important, because it potentially changes the whole playing field. Targeting ambitious new product functionalities, especially in new market segments, has the potential to add truly incremental revenue streams to your business, negating the constraints applied by your existing market dynamics, and if you have done your planning well enough, launching you into a market leading position compared to your competitors, irrespective of M&A activity.

Inorganic Growth

1) Advantages – in contrast to organic growth, one of the great advantages of taking an inorganic investment route to growth is that it can deliver really quick results. If you acquire another company, whilst the planning, negotiation and due diligence will take some time to work through of course, once the legal aspects of the acquisition are completed, the financials of your new acquisition can get consolidated into your own business right away. This means your sales are going to see an immediate upswing. It's essentially the same for a merger, with the combined entity automatically delivering bigger revenues, and additionally, the larger size of either type of combined entity allows for better cash flow control and a stronger line of credit to take on debt financing because of the larger customer base, higher value of assets and bigger market presence. Depending on the relative size of the other business you are acquiring or merging with, you could potentially be looking at a doubling of your customer list and revenues, or more. The automatic increase in market share comes with a whole new set of channels to market for you, and the added benefit of existing relationships with customers that were previously not your own, putting you in a much stronger position to build further market presence, especially given that the acquisition, merger or joint venture also adds new expertise and experience from the

personnel in the other business. If you make the right choice of target for your acquisition, merger or partnership, and manage the implementation effectively, then all of these advantages add up to realigning your business into a much better competitive position, giving you a serious step up in the market place, and a stronger position from which to call the shots in terms of pricing. This places you in an even better position for future growth. Whether through acquisition or merger, combining businesses which have some commonality in manufacturing processes, product technologies and/or an overlap in geographical markets served also offers the potential for cost reduction, through bulk purchasing agreements, overhead consolidation and downsizing to improve profitability. Note that the latter comes with considerable implementation challenges (see "disadvantages" below). Combining businesses which have complementary, but not overlapping, products, and routes to market and operations, offers further growth potential in the form of combining product groups to extend the service offering to the wider customer base, the possibility of introducing existing products into new markets, and enhanced innovation opportunities by bringing together technologies to create something new to the market.

2) Disadvantages – the flipside to the great advantage of speed of delivery that inorganic growth options can offer, is that this comes with a much larger associated risk and a much higher upfront cost. Combining two existing businesses, whether through acquisition, merger or joint venture is a huge management challenge, and very difficult to get right. You are dealing with two existing businesses, each of which will have their own employees, their own working culture, and their own ways of doing things. The employees will have loyalties to their current business and in most cases will view the other business as a competitor in their market. All this means that come the time for integration of the two businesses – whatever form it will take – the barriers will go up in many parts of the two businesses, and with many individuals, plenty of whom will resist the change, either actively or passively. Not only do you need to project manage the integration of the two businesses in an operational way – looking at all aspects of how best to combine the management structures, the different business processes, the operational footprint,

the sales and distribution channels, not to mention branding decisions – you will also need to launch a change management project to ease people through the massive upheaval that may be coming their way. As mentioned in the previous section, combining businesses can frequently lead to redeployment of personnel into new roles and/or to redundancies, as job functions, back office services and functional departments are merged. The associated overhead saving this can deliver is indeed one of the benefits that business owners and management expect to get out of the deal in the first place. With an acquisition, you can normally expect it's the personnel in the company that is being acquired that will get affected the most, as the lead management team tend to naturally want to stick with their own existing team when making the difficult personnel choices. With mergers, it's not such a cut-and-dried scenario, with plenty of behind-the-scenes boardroom battles required before the dominant board members emerge. Joint ventures tend to be very different situations, because a JV is normally an additive business, opening up a new territory or market, and so the two existing businesses are not so greatly affected. That's not to say JVs are not without their own management and integration challenges, as JVs are usually seeded with employees from each of the partner companies, who each have allegiances to their parent company, plus a smattering of new employees, who normally build allegiance to the JV. So people management in a JV in such a rich and complex environment requires its own unique approach. Whether acquisition, merger or JV, whilst the deal can be done relatively quickly, and financials consolidated positively, the reality on the ground is that getting to the point that the new entity is fully combined, personnel are fully integrated and the new business is working effectively and efficiently can take many years. In fact, it can be just as long as delivering one of the organic growth routes. And all along the way, achieving the integration necessary to fully reap the benefit of the investment will be being undermined by those who actively, or passively, resist the changes, piling an enormous risk onto your investment. Consolidation of two businesses can be a very painful experience for many, so you should not enter into it lightly. It is going to require a lot of management time and energy and all the interpersonal skills you can muster to make a success of it.

And the reality is, in the absence of a plan, dedicated resources and without a clear project owner, plenty of acquisitions remain poorly integrated for many years, sometimes decades. I have worked in businesses where I saw this happen, where employees at individual sites, acquired 20 years previously, still did not consider themselves as part of the owner's group of businesses, still used their own branding, and had very little interaction with parent and sister companies within the group. Sure, the financials were consolidated into the owner's, but there were none of the additional benefits of integration realised at the time. Successful integration of businesses will only happen with buy-in from both parties, and that can only happen with hard work, strong leadership and a well-resourced plan. Another risk that occurs when combining two existing businesses, is that your existing management may not be up to the challenge; after all, you may be creating an entity that is on a far grander scale and level of complexity than any of your existing management have the experience of dealing with before. There could be far greater numbers of employees to deal with, new territories they are unfamiliar with, and a broader set of assets to manage. So the management team may require training to upskill, bringing in outside specialist support, or in some cases, replacing with a more experienced individual, all to make sure the business is up to the task of integration. There are also strategic risks, the new business you create may grow in ways you had not expected and enter markets where the leadership team have no expertise, which can challenge and force the team to question the strategic vision for the new company. Growth may even outstrip your ability to finance it, particularly as inorganic growth investment usually requires higher upfront costs compared to organic routes, and this will normally be externally financed, burdening the new entity with debt that will need to be covered by the growth delivered by the acquisition, merger or JV. Grow faster than you planned for and your new business can quickly run out of money, and so putting in place robust financial processes and a strong finance team are crucial in minimising the risk of making inorganic growth investments.

So I hope you have no doubt now: innovation, in the form of new product development, and all the various aspects that covers, including R&D, is a major investment for any business, just like building a new factory, just like making an acquisition. And if you were laying down serious cash to build a factory or make an acquisition, you would measure and monitor those investments carefully, wouldn't you? You would assign a dedicated manger, who was clearly and solely responsible for delivering that investment project. You would put in tight project management systems and you would regularly review progress at board level. So why don't all companies do the same with their innovation investment? Why is new product development not treated in the same way? When you consider the level of investment, they are frequently on the same scale. Investing $200k every year over five years to develop a new product is of the same magnitude as spending $1m on a new factory extension. Investing $10m a year on new product development over five years could build you a brand-new factory. So why is new product development not measured so carefully by many businesses? It is back to themes I touched on in *Transforming Technology into Profit* – it is due to the lack of understanding of the role that innovation plays in a business at the very top. It is the frequent attitude from CEOs and CFOs, that it's just science: let the geeks dabble and come up with something new. Innovation too frequently does not get a mention at the top table. So, whilst the board is busy reviewing progress on its capital investment project, checking whether the budget is on track, it too frequently glosses over the same scale of investment it is making behind the scenes in trying to grow through new products. Where are the innovation metrics, where are the key performance indicators (KPIs), where are the targets? This is what this book is really about, trying to explain and simplify the process of innovation for business leadership.

I hope you have a better understanding and appreciation now of the fact that innovation and R&D has to stand up and prove itself against competing forms of investment if it is to get funded by a business. If you are the one responsible for technology in your business, you can see that you are up against significant internal competition to get your innovation work funded, and in many businesses that is unfortunately the situation you find yourself, in which case you will be spending an awful lot of time working the politics. Of course, if the CEO and board of the company prioritise innovation goals above all else for the business, it will make your life so much easier in terms of getting the funding and resources you need to deliver.

What Exactly Is the Innovation Industry?

We have established that in the process of innovation that businesses need to work through in order to create ideas, develop those ideas into projects, select the best projects and implement them through to scale-up, productionisation and successful commercialisation is very well known. But if these processes are so well known and understood, how come 89% of businesses are still struggling to grow? (See earlier in this chapter). And it is not as if these businesses don't have support. Apart from the skilled, experienced and talented management teams leading them, there is a vast array of external support services freely available to all of these businesses, and they come in many forms. They all tend to come under the banner of "innovation", they all claim to be "innovation" companies and most have the word in their company name and/or marketing tagline, but in fact they are all focusing on different aspects of the process of innovation, which adds further complexity and confusion to the field. In working for so many years in this area, I have interacted with many of these so called "innovation" companies, and they can be categorised into one of four main types:

1) *Ideation* support companies – These types of "innovation" companies focus on what's called the "fuzzy front end'" of the innovation process – the area that cannot be completely managed with spreadsheets and business processes because this is the part where the ideas are created. These types of companies are usually non-industry specific, and work with individuals and groups to help them be more creative. They essentially teach general idea creation techniques, and usually have their own methods to get individuals and teams to be more creative and to come up with more and better ideas. These are usually taught and practised through practical workshop style training events.
2) *Start-up* support companies – These types of "innovation" companies help small start-ups to grow their business or help individuals and teams to get their business idea off the ground by linking them to government start-up or innovation grants and/or to university R&D departments or partner companies to help them develop their ideas and technology further to commercialisation.
3) *Process step* support companies – These types of "innovation" companies focus on one or more of the innovation process steps, and tend

to be specialised in either idea management, project management or portfolio management. They all bring their own approach and best practice to these essential business processes, though this more often than not boils down to trying to sell you their bespoke software, which they claim makes the whole process much more efficient, speeding up communication and decision-making. Whilst this may or may not be true, the real issue I have with these companies is when they try to sell this under the banner of innovation, as if such software will solve all your innovation problems. In my experience – and I have worked with (and been involved with developing) many different idea, project and portfolio business processes (including software versions) – yes, you can and should strive to improve all your systems, but even the most basic, least sophisticated of processes are usually good enough to work with and build an efficient innovation process off. It is no good focusing all your time and energy on building a better project management system if the problem holding back your business' ability to grow through new products is not your project management system. Building a better mousetrap is not much use if you don't have a problem with mice. This is also the area you will likely first come into contact with so called "Agile" techniques, which grew out of the software industry. And for the same reason as above, I find the endless "waterfall" versus "Agile" debate all rather pointless (remember that "waterfall" is just another name for the phase-gate approach). The constant arguments about which approach is best for project management seems to largely have been perpetuated by companies trying to sell their Agile software or to get people trained and certified in Agile techniques, i.e. it is simply a marketing activity. What started out as a great philosophy and way of getting teams to work together, share common goals and prioritise practical approaches seems to have been hijacked by some businesses to build Agile into a brand, rather than an approach to working, which in my experience has only served to divide the business community and detract from its value. And worse than this, in some cases Agile has been blown out of all proportion and is hyped by some as the epitome of modern business approaches, a suite of tools to transform every aspect of a business to attain some kind of organisational nirvana. I will expand more on this subject in Chapter 3.

4) *Full process* support companies – These types of "innovation" companies come under the banner of general management consulting companies. They are essentially departments within the big global management consultancy companies: Bain and Company, Boston Consulting Group, L.E.K. Consulting, A.T. Kearney, etc. Some of the world's biggest multinational companies (e.g. BASF) also have their own internal departments or stand-alone businesses performing a similar task. I have worked with several of these "big" consulting companies over the years and sat through umpteen strategy reviews facilitated by such companies. In almost every business I have worked, every two or three years the company board would choose to do a strategy review, and certainly it was always initiated by every new CEO that was appointed. Quite right you say, absolutely, it is important for any business to take regular stock of the direction in which it is heading and plot its path to growth. But what actually happens in these processes? After the decision was taken to start a strategic review, the next step would be to call in a cross-section of the top management consulting firms and preside over a "beauty parade" of their teams. One by one they would stroll in, and we would spend a whole day sitting through all their pitches, listening to how they can help us grow. We would choose the firm we want to work with, negotiate the price and then launch into the strategic review proper. It depends on the size and complexity of your business, but typically the firm would assign a team of three to five consultants, presided over by one or more senior consultants with a couple of associated partners thrown in for expert advice, and the review process would be run as a tightly managed project over several weeks. In reality, the team of consultants assigned to your project are typically a bunch of very intelligent, but relatively inexperienced new graduates who seem to work 20 hours a day on your project over the next few weeks: pulling together information, analysing market data and collating PowerPoint presentations. This is all in preparation for the regular update reviews, at which the senior consultant rarely appears in person – just over the phone – and in which the partners, the ones with the real experience, that were dangled in front of you during the pitch, are rarely involved. And how much do you typically pay for the privilege of all this? Half a million dollars? Sometimes much more. Sure, the process and the

> tight deadline forces you to spit out a new, revised business strategy at the end of it, but I refer you back to the 89% of businesses that are still struggling to grow. So whilst these big consulting firms certainly bring masses of valuable market data to the process, you have to question the value of the strategy that is produced in this way. Sure, the process is a two-way street and yes, delivering growth is equally about the effectiveness of implementation of the strategy, not just the quality of the strategy in the first place, which is certainly down to the business, not the consulting firm. But still, the whole process has always felt rather unsatisfactory to me, and to many of my colleagues, and certainly an incredibly overpriced one for what comes out of it. Yet businesses all over the planet still keep going through this same process, again and again. There has to be a better way. And when it comes to the typical big consulting firms' approach to helping companies improve their innovation process, this has been described to me by one of my colleagues as "R&D by numbers". The same type of young, inexperienced team is assigned to your company to teach you about how to do innovation, and it's just a textbook approach of walking through the classic steps of idea generation, idea selection, project management and commercialisation. These people have never had to implement these processes themselves in a real company. They may know the process they are explaining intimately, but if they do not have the experience to understand and appreciate that there are other "internal factors" at play that can make or break the standard process of innovation, then how can they hope to truly make a difference to growing the business? This is, after all, the point of having an innovation process. This is the fundamental problem with using external consultants as advisors when those advising have never had to actually take charge themselves and implement something. Sure, there are individual exceptions, but in my experience, ratified by feedback from my colleagues, these are the exceptions, not the norm.

How can so many different types of companies all be "innovation" companies? How is it helpful to all use the same banner to ply their trade? How does this differentiate them and their business from their competitors? This is the practical reality of how confusing the market has become in looking for support and how business certainly appreciates the importance of innovation but is still struggling with finding a clear coherent approach to it.

So, if all this external support is out there, and has been around for many years, how come we still have 89% of businesses struggling to grow? Presumably many of these businesses have been making use of at least some of these external support services. I know the businesses I worked in over the years used several of these services and worked with many of these consultancy companies. And if these supporting companies are so good at what they do, and if (presumably) they make demonstrable improvements in the businesses with which they work (they wouldn't survive very long as businesses if they didn't), then how come we still have the 89% figure? If these supporting services were truly making a difference, surely the percentage of companies struggling to grow would be much, much lower. The answer is that in each case, they are only addressing part of the issue. In each case, they are only making a difference to one aspect of the challenge of innovation in a business. And whilst they may achieve improvements to that one aspect in the businesses they are working with, if the particular aspect of the process of innovation they are improving is not the one that is holding back the business from delivering new products, then it is not going to make much of a contribution to helping the business grow. And whilst the effort may seem to deliver a positive and worthwhile outcome, in reality it has been rather a waste of time and money. Unless you really understand what things in your business are truly holding back the ability of your business to deliver innovation, then your approach is going to simply be a scatter-gun one. You might get lucky and happen to work on the real issue, but since, as we will see later in this book, there are just so many things that need to work together effectively for a business to grow through new products, then it is rather unlikely you will choose to work on the real bottleneck just by luck. So I am not saying that all of these support service companies are useless at what they do, or pointless in their approach, what I am saying is that they only address one or two specific aspects of innovation in a business, so on their own they are very unlikely to be able to deliver what your business really needs if it wants to unlock its potential for innovation and grow through new products. To do this effectively, you need to take a truly holistic approach to how innovation works in a business and identify and target the true barriers. But how do you do that? Well, read on.

References

Castellion, G. & Markham., S. K. 2013. New Product Failure Rates: Influence of Argumentum ad Populum and Self-Interest. *Journal of Product Innovation & Management* 30(5): 976–979.

Schroeder, Kurt. 2017. Why so many new products fail (and it's not the product). Bizjournals.com. https://www.bizjournals.com/bizjournals/how-to/marketing/2017/03/why-so-many-new-products-fail-and-it-s-not-the.html#:~:text=According%20to%20Harvard%20Business%20School,80%20percent%20of%20them%20fail

Stevens, G. A. & Burley, J. 1997. 3,000 Raw Ideas = 1 Commercial Success!, *Research Technology Management* 40(3): 1601–1703.

2

THE INNOVATION JOURNEY

> Innovation is a business process that requires active engagement by all functions, certainly R&D, but also Finance, Marketing, Sales, Operations, Legal, CEO and Board, any one of whom can destroy the hard work of the other functions.
>
> Cliff Spiro, Chief Technology Officer at Entrepix Medical

My Own Innovation Journey

As I stated at the start of Chapter 1, innovation has been my life. I have spent 30 years continuously learning about the whole process, sometimes from the position of leading new product development initiatives, sometimes from the position of running businesses and needing to add new revenue streams to grow, and I am still learning today.

My innovation journey started out like many technologists, I expect: working in a laboratory, developing new technologies and new products. I didn't start out with any great desire to build a career out of technology, that particular passion developed later in my career. I studied chemistry at university because I was good at it. It wasn't that other subjects didn't interest me, it's just that I always got the best marks at school in the science subjects, and in chemistry in particular. So I did what I thought was the most sensible thing to do when I left school and followed what I seemed to excel at. It wasn't that science particularly excited me any more than art subjects, I guess I just thought there would be a better chance of getting a decent pay packet from a more practical subject out in the real world. And I certainly tried to avoid the real world as long as I could. That's one of the reasons I stayed at university for six years: three years as an undergraduate, three years as a postgraduate. I loved student life, and it taught me many broader things about life as a young adult, not just the academic side of my education. Another reason I stayed on after my degree was that I thought it would be really cool, and more bankable job-wise, to have a PhD and get to call myself "Doctor". I since learnt later on, as my career grew internationally, that that seems to be a particularly British thing, as in the US they just put the letters PhD after their name, and someone with "Doctor" in front of their name tends to be considered a Medical Doctor, and adds MD after their name. I knew throughout my studies that I eventually wanted to go out into industry and put my education to practical use, rather than stay in academia. Once my six years of being a student finally came to an end and I had to look for a real job out in the scary world of adults, I did the usual rounds of corporate interviews. The job market was reasonably buoyant in those days. I had 21 interviews and got offered jobs by six different companies, a pretty good hit rate. I specialised in inorganic chemistry for my PhD, which inevitably dictated the types of companies I was interviewing with and the choice of first job I eventually decided to take. This was the starting point for a career route that took me into the advanced materials and industrial engineering industry.

During my PhD, I was sponsored by the UK Atomic Energy Authority to develop organic molecules to selectively capture cobalt ions from pressurised water reactor cooling water systems. The problem I was trying to solve was that cobalt was being leached out of the steel pipework by corrosion mechanisms, entering the cooling water and flowing past the reactor core, rendering the cobalt ions radioactive, with the potential to travel out beyond the core zone, depositing radioactivity in corrosion deposits throughout the cooling water system, and the UKAEA wanted to develop technology to control it and minimise the risk. So I was already starting to use my technical skills for practical purposes, though in the case of my PhD, not really within a business environment.

My first real job was as a senior technologist at the R&D Centre of a global multinational advanced material manufacturer, and I was put to work on developing tin oxide sensor materials, piezoceramic composites, and other electroceramic-related projects. This first job is when I took my first real step on a career long innovation journey. What I started to learn about in these first formative years working on practical material and product development was essentially the skill of project management: having to plan work, set targets, work with colleagues, communicate progress, etc. I was quickly moved into a new role, heading up the refractory materials group at the R&D centre, and given a small team to manage. During those first few years, I worked on a continuous stream of product development projects, working with companies all over the world within the group and with end users in multiple industries, all the time learning and improving my project management skills and starting to look outside of my own environment to learn how others tackled project management.

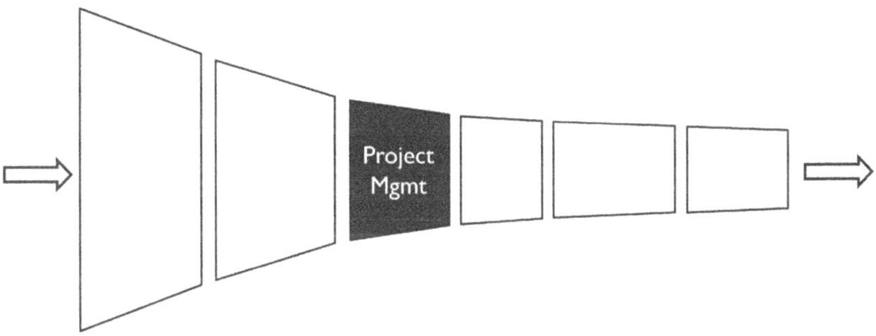

As my team and I started to have success on certain projects in the laboratory and out in the field with prototypes, we were then tasked with having to start scaling up our successful new technologies and products. This is when we started working more closely for the first time with process engineers and learning the challenges of expanding technologies up to the pilot scale. It was quite an eye-opener as a young technologist to discover that all that smart work you had done at the bench scale wasn't enough to get that new product out. You think you've done all the hard work and the rest should be plain sailing. It is quite astounding the new challenges that arise when you try to recreate the same technology at a larger scale, things you never considered at the bench. Not least you have to consider are things like handling and mixing of bulk materials, a much wider range of health and safety aspects and many other practicalities that rarely come into play during the initial development phase. And you start having to set limits for measured properties and trying to get your new technology to behave within these limits. Really not easy. And you start to appreciate that scale-up really is a different phase of the innovation process, requiring a different, broader set of skills.

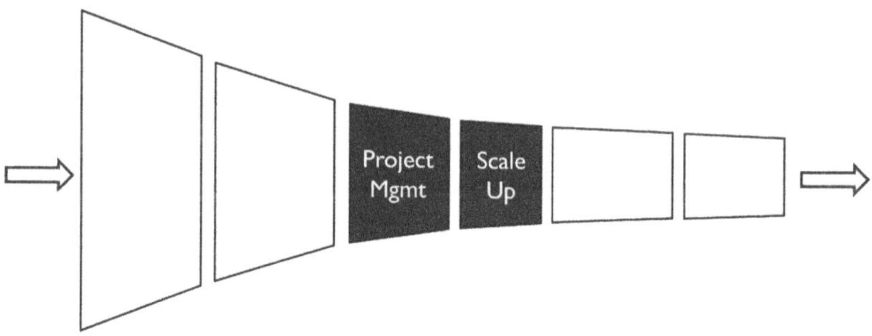

As I pushed on through the challenges of scale-up, after considerable hard work, team effort and a little luck, some of our projects did pass successfully through and we found our new technologies and new products meeting all the targets we set for scale-up. This is when I was introduced properly to the next phase of the innovation process: productionisation. This is where you and your team, along with your new process engineering friends, start to work closely with the production team, with production management, with operators and with the quality control team. This is where you take your scaled-up technology onto a fully functioning, full-scale production line. Depending on the scale of your business, this may mean working with people in the same building, or it might mean working with a team in a different country, on the other side of the planet, which presents a whole new set of logistical and cultural challenges. In my case, it was usually the latter, as the R&D Centre was not affiliated directly with a manufacturing site. This phase in particular starts to open up your eyes not only to the considerable technical challenges of shoehorning your technology into a full-scale production line, but also to a whole range of influencing and people skills that need to come into play, trying to schedule your production trials in amongst existing production schedules. It is a harsh reality to learn that your new product development project is not the most important thing in the business and that other people have their own priorities.

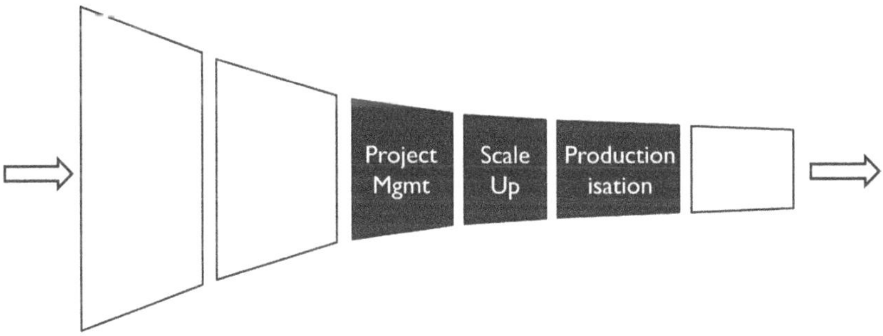

As time went on in my career, and projects progressed, some of the projects I worked on fortunately passed successfully through the unique challenges of productionisation. It is a satisfying feeling when your new product can be made repeatedly, cost effectively and at scale. It feels a real achievement for you and the team, one worth celebrating. It is then you move on to the next phase of your innovation journey, and you get to work more closely with the sales and marketing team on full commercialisation of the new product. I had of course been working with some sales people along my journey already, and with some end users during product trials, but as you start to work towards an official product launch, I discovered that a much larger group of the sales team tends to become involved, and the breadth and extent of customer trials grow to the point that you cannot be involved in all of them, and you have to start training the sales team in the use of the new products. This is where the table turned for them and for myself, and I finally had to learn to hand over ownership of "my" new product to others. This "letting go" was a difficult time for me, a real education in maturity, but I also discovered it is a huge challenge when those that need to take ownership for successful handover don't want to (which is usually the case) or at least don't feel comfortable doing it until it has been made foolproof, with zero risk to them (which is never realistically going to happen, even with all the FMEAs [Failure Mode and Effects Analyses] in the world). What I came to realise after my first few commercialisation experiences, was that there is a massive set of people and behavioural problems to deal with during this phase of the innovation journey, more new skills to learn, and another step towards personal maturity that is required to work successfully through it.

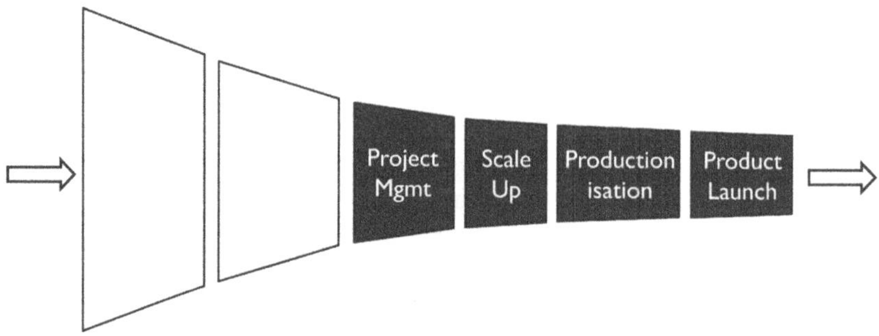

The first time I was involved in a new product development project that led to successful commercialisation was an incredible feeling, a huge sense of achievement. There are certainly several other steps along the way down the innovation journey that are also great accomplishments, when you achieve major milestones, and I learnt that it is important to recognise and celebrate these. This is, after all, how you maintain momentum and get through a multi-year project, and I learnt that this is an important method of motivating the team – and yourself – to keep going. And once you have achieved commercial success with a new product you were assigned to develop, of course the business wants to assign you more such projects, and give you more responsibility, and so you get to do it all over again, and go through the same steps of project management, scale-up, productionisation and commercialisation. Only this time you get to do if with a promotion, and a bigger team, and with more projects to manage.

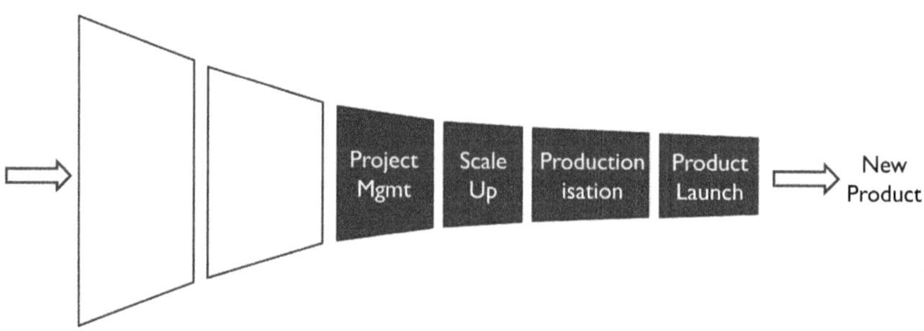

At this point in my career, with multiple projects to handle, this was when I first became exposed to portfolio management and started to learn how to juggle different priorities within the various projects. This was my first official management role, and the natural consequence of delivering tangible results that I anticipated in my career at that point. But management is not for everyone. Some people that start off their careers in a technical role are totally comfortable with continuing that, and that is what they want to focus the rest of their career on. They don't want to broaden their responsibilities into people management and into the mechanics of running a business, they want to use their technical skills to solve technical problems – that's what drives them, that's what interests them. And so "technical specialist" is a career path that needs to be recognised and appreciated for the value that these people bring to a business. But I knew early on that was not a route I wanted to go down. Just as I realised during my university studies that I wanted to do more practical things with science, develop technologies and products that made a difference to people, a similar recognition dawned on me during my first few years in the company R&D centre. I had learnt much about applying technology to solve the practical challenges of a wide variety of customers, in several different industry sectors, but my innovation journey had also taught me that technology is not the only skill you need to make this happen. It had shown me that to transform technology into a successful product, you need process and production engineering skills, sales and marketing skills, people management skills, influencing and negotiation skills, customer engagement skills. And in fact, I came to appreciate that you need to bring almost all parts of a business to bear in order to make this happen. It was at this point in my career that I knew I could never truly achieve this satisfactorily sitting in an R&D Centre, I needed to be in a real business, in amongst the thick of it, interfacing directly with all departments. And so I decided to find a more suitable role out in a business, one where I could build on what I had learnt already and take my innovation journey to the next level.

My first move out of the corporate R&D Centre, from a largely R&D/technical environment, into a real business, was as technical manager for a £50m turnover global division, making consumables and equipment for the ferrous and non-ferrous foundry market. I had been working with this business more and more closely during my R&D centre days, so it was a natural and comfortable progression for all involved. I already knew the technology, I knew the people and I knew the markets. The division had several small to medium manufacturing sites and sales offices around the world, in North and South America, right across Europe, Asia and Australasia, with a strong supporting network of distributors and agents. It proved to be a smart move for me and an ideal environment in which to learn broader management skills and continue my innovation journey, because with around 500 employees globally, it meant that responsibilities were distributed broadly, and I got to take ownership of many more functions than I had originally anticipated or expected.

Once inside the business as technical manager, I found myself working through much the same innovation and project management processes I had experienced in the earlier R&D environment, but I soon realised that sitting on the other side of the fence meant that not only did I have to deliver the projects, I now had to take responsibility for coming up with the projects in the first place, to feed the innovation machine for the business and keep it in the market-leading position it enjoyed in the future. This was a very different dynamic, and led me to appreciate that I had to engage with multiple business functions to a deeper, more strategic level, talking with sales, marketing, the executive team, the customer base, and many more, to build up a list of ideas from which to create potential new product development projects for the business. This is where I first got to start working on the input side of the innovation process. I had spent my formative career years learning how to manage projects through to their successful commercial conclusion (the output side of the equation), and now I was learning about how to generate and manage ideas (the input side).

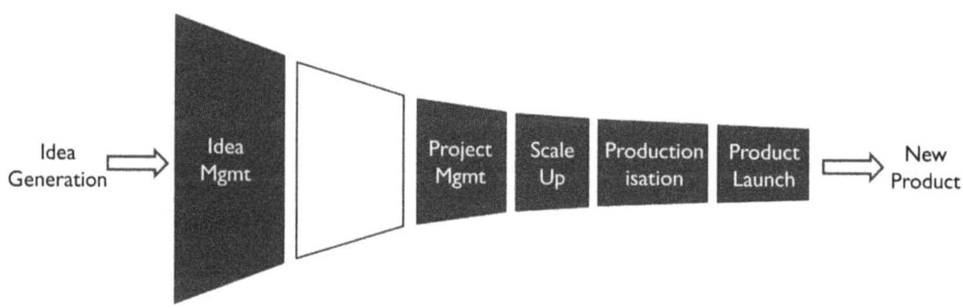

Once I became better at probing people for input, gathering ideas and putting them into some kind of logical order, rather than just creating a mind dump, I then had to learn to do something with all these ideas. It was then that I began to work on systems for idea selection, to try to choose those ideas that had the best potential for commercial gain for the business, and I discovered that it was not easy. Once inside a real business, I began to appreciate that there are many more factors that need to be taken into account when making a judgement call on which ideas to run with and which to shelve. Financial considerations, intellectual property risks and strategic direction of the business – they all featured much more prominently in my thinking than they had when I sat outside of the loop in the R&D Centre. And organising senior management to work methodically through a selection process, rather than just listen to "he who shouts loudest", was a significant challenge in influencing and negotiation skills.

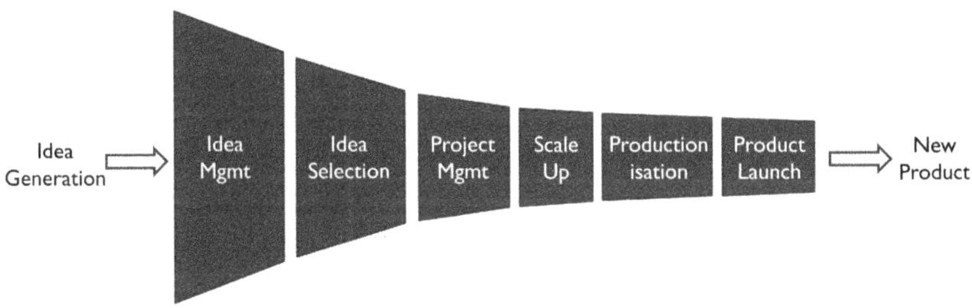

By then, I was around ten years into my career since starting as a technologist fresh from university, and what had I learnt? I didn't know it at the time, but what I had actually learnt was the "innovation funnel". After ten years, I had finally been exposed to, and taken charge of, each step of the now classic process of generating ideas, selecting ideas, managing projects, scaling up, commercialising and launching new products. So, now I had it all down pat. The process was clear. I was an expert, right? By then I had basic systems in place for managing each of the steps and delivering outputs. So, I should have started to get more and more, and better and better new products out to grow the business, right? Sure, I was certainly more experienced by then. I better appreciated the diversity of inputs that needed to be taken into account, the complexity of skills and approaches that needed to be brought to bear at different phases of the process and the inherent levels of risk underlying each phase. But it all still seemed much tougher than it ought to be, it was still too often a frustrating experience working with all the different individuals and teams, keeping everyone on track and keeping it all together.

So I thought: my process must be flawed, or not good enough, too inefficient. So as I worked through my job as technical manager, and then as technical director after I got promoted, I started to focus on improving all the processes one by one, reading more on the subject, attending seminars, getting external consultancy help and advice where necessary, and streamlining and derisking the whole innovation process we had in place. I spent a lot of time updating checklists, refining spreadsheets, rewriting phase-gate documents with my team, sometimes with external support, in a bid to continuously improve the whole innovation process. And it was also during that time that I was starting to spread my wings beyond my core technical functions, taking on responsibilities for other functions in the business. I took on responsibility for process control, for health and safety, for communications, and eventually on into general management. It had always been a career goal of mine to work my way up the corporate ladder into business management. But in so doing, I naively believed that that would be the end of my innovation journey, that if I moved on to business management, I would be handing over the "job" of innovation on to my replacement. However, by the time I took on my first general manager role, leading an OEM business designing and making furnaces, I felt I had built a great understanding of the innovation process and a great system to manage it all, so I felt comfortable moving onwards and upwards in my career to my next challenge.

Once in a general manager role, I started juggling all the key functions, finance, sales administration, operations, even going out on the road doing sales calls myself, trying to learn first-hand the particular skills and challenges of each. But despite what I had anticipated, I found I could never really leave innovation behind. Even though I had a different team of technical experts running the mechanics of the process itself, it was a real learning experience for me just how much the business leader still had to be involved in innovation and take it seriously if it was to really work – after all, it was the future of the business, so it could not be left to chance. It had to be integrated fully into the continuous programme of activities running to streamline business processes, reduce costs, improve efficiencies and grow sales, all wrapped up in a clear and coherent strategy and implementation plan. And this is the period in my career that I began to appreciate just how important the person at the top is in driving and delivering new products to grow the business. It wasn't like it happened over night of course, it took me many years in business leadership roles, from general manager, through managing a small global division, then a large global division, before I finally came to appreciate this, all the time learning bit by bit.

But it wasn't just through inward reflection and learning: all along the way I had my own boss to answer to of course, and so I also learnt from them. Over a 30-year career, I have had ten bosses, all very different people, with different styles of leadership, different strengths and weaknesses and different backgrounds and preferences. Some of my bosses were very much of the view that innovation was someone else's role, not something they needed to get involved with, and that they could delegate it 100%. When I had a boss like that, they might have technology and new product development updates tagged on to the end of a two-day board meeting agenda, but we would inevitably run out of time in our discussions and never get round to talking about it. Other bosses I worked for would have a much stronger opinion on the importance of technology in delivering the future and would have a whole day of the board meeting devoted to it.

This was also the period of my career when I could start to see how innovation fitted into a business in a more holistic sense. Once new product development was not my individual responsibility, I could better observe how technology as a function interacted with other functions in a business. This is why I say today that I have experienced innovation from both sides of the technology fence: firstly as a practitioner, as the person responsible for delivering new products and processes, and then, as a business leader, with responsibility for delivering on P&L. This is truly when I started to see all the friction, the politics, the lack of ownership, lack of effective project handover, and many, many more negative behaviours and personal interactions that could bring down innovation and slow or halt progress of new product development projects. This was where I acquired much of the subject matter that became my first book, *Transforming Technology into Profit*.

Over the next few years of operational management and business leadership roles, during the middle period of my career, I began to see how business functions naturally had crossover points, and to appreciate more that teams from different departments had to work together in order to make things happen. This is where I developed my first embryonic understanding of collaborative innovation organisations and of functional interfaces, which eventually developed into the models that featured in my first book, reprinted below.

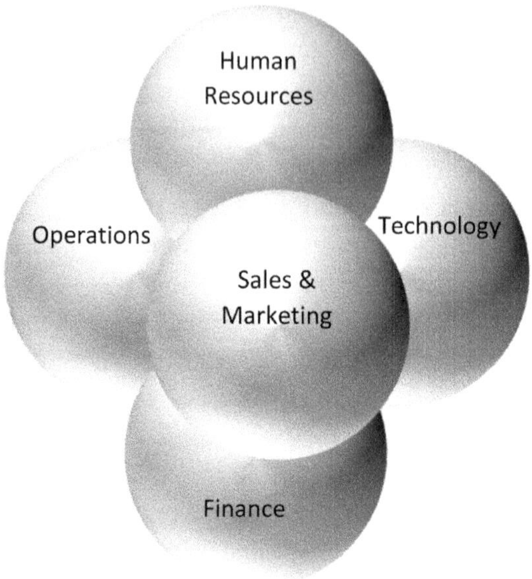

As the scale and reach of my general management roles grew into bigger and bigger businesses, reaching ever more diverse markets and geographies, and on up the corporate ladder, eventually I took the natural next career step out of operational management into strategic management. One of the significant personal challenges of operational management is that it is an extremely time absorbing and extremely stressful role. Having accountability for delivering P&L targets every month, every quarter, every year, is a responsibility that weighs heavy on anyone's shoulders, and is not for the fainthearted. The responsibilities are far reaching. It's not just your job and career future on the line, it is the jobs and livelihoods of everyone employed in the business(es) for which you are responsible that are at stake. For many in such a role, it absorbs your whole waking hours, eats heavily into your personal and family time, and increasingly takes up your weekends. It is a heavy price to pay, particularly for those with young families, and achieving a good work-life balance is almost impossible. You do it for the money of course, the rewards, to build financial security for your family. It's a matter of personal choice whether it's worth it, but it is a normal part of corporate career progression. If you have found yourself in this type of P&L role, you will know how hard it is to find any time to stop and look at the bigger picture, to take time to do the strategic planning that is really needed to guide the business in the right direction, so often you find yourself dragged into the day-to-day crises that constantly emerge. It's a matter of delegation to some extent, but it still takes a lot of self-discipline and courage to step away from the day to day, when the bottom line sits at your feet. Moving to a strategic role, with longer term goals and the chance and the jurisdiction to look at the bigger picture, finally gives you that time. There are still plenty of regular reporting demands and office politics to deal with – those are still there at any level of business – so it's still not easy, but it was only really once I moved to a strategic role and sat outside the operational day-to-day processes of running a business, that I had the opportunity to start to see and understand properly the full situation of how innovation works in a business environment.

My transition from operational management to strategic management was not actually a straight line because I first took a sideways step: I moved to China to build a factory. My business was looking for someone to set up a joint venture in China that they had just invested in, and it was in a part of the business that I knew really well, so they offered me the chance to go out and set the whole thing up, on a greenfield site in the North East of China, in a city called Dalian. What a great opportunity to bring all of the management and business skills that I had picked up over the years together! It was not innovation in the sense of new product development, as this book is focused around, but it certainly involved innovation in a broader sense, because we had to design a new production process, so there was plenty of creativity and new engineering design to be done.

What an incredible opportunity to be offered, a blank sheet of paper on which to design and bring to life a brand-new manufacturing business. How many times does an opportunity like that come your way in a corporate career? And to do it halfway round the world in a country and a culture that is so different from the West. I grabbed it with both hands. A scary prospect for sure, but incredibly exciting. I was under no illusion that it was going to be a walk in the park, I fully expected it to be a minefield of politics and cultural challenges and I was not wrong. Even just trying to live your life in China as an expat is a daily personal challenge, and one which inspired me to write another of my books – check out *The Biggest City You've Never Heard Of*, about living and doing business as an expat in China.

So, I became Project Director for building the new factory and setting up the new business, a role that called on all my technical, managerial and interpersonal skills. It was a unique environment within which to project manage civil engineering work, manage local government relationships and the relationship with the joint venture partners, ensure the availability of funding, and design and staff a whole new organisation for the company. But I could not have done it all on my own: the first thing I had to do was build up a new team to oversee all the different aspects of the project – electrical and mechanical engineering, building approvals, works management and sourcing all the construction and equipment suppliers we would need. I was lucky to have a great team, a mixture of local Chinese with some foreign experts. The project was certainly not plain sailing: a story full of plot twists, cliff hangers, nasty behind-the-scenes politics, and brushes with the local mafia, that probably warrants a book all of its own, but we got there in the end.

After completion of my first China project, I stepped up to my first big strategic role, as Technical Director for the Asian region, but throughout this time, I did not entirely leave my Project Director role behind, as I went on to lead or support several other factory builds and joint venture negotiations in China and within the wider Asian region. The Asian region, for our business, basically covered half the planet, from the Middle East down to Australasia, so I spent an awful lot of my time on an airplane and sitting in airports. An occupational hazard, but worth it for the chance to experience so many different cultures and new countries. Throughout this role I remained based in China – after all, it represented half of our Asian region sales and was the market with the biggest growth opportunities, and so was an excellent base of operations for me. And even when I was promoted to become the Chief Technology Officer for our whole global division, I still stayed living in China. Why? Because in spite of the initial scariness of moving halfway round the world to start a new life, the truth was that my wife and I loved China, we thrived there. It was such a vibrant, stimulating and positive environment within which to live and do business, and I learnt a lot about myself, both personally and professionally in my six years there. Stepping out of your normal working environment into somewhere so different, so alien, forces you to test yourself in ways you had never imagined, forces you into situations and confrontations that are extremely uncomfortable, and at times, downright dangerous. But you push through, you learn to adapt and the experience drives you to mature and develop personal resilience far quicker than would have occurred if you'd stayed back in your comfy corporate existence.

Throughout my strategic management roles, I was still part of a big global multinational, and so I had colleagues in other divisions of the business, who like me, were responsible for innovation, technology and new product development in their division. It was great to be able to work with a bunch of like-minded individuals, we had a lot of fun together, achieved a lot and it was a privilege to work with them all. One of the things we did together was to go back to basics and build a common innovation process that the whole of the multinational business could use, so that we were all using the same approach, the same tools, and the same reporting methodologies. This gave me the opportunity yet again in my career to dig down into the detail of the innovation funnel and refine the full set of management tools summarised in Chapter 1. It was amazing to see how different parts of the same group had evolved different styles of innovation tools over the years. Such exercises had been done before in the global business, but every time you get people together to agree a common set of tools, checklists, spreadsheet, etc., if you do not appoint someone to manage the whole thing from that point on, then you must expect it all to drift off in different directions again. Everyone thinks they know better, everyone wants to tweak it a little bit, and a little bit more, and there are subtle differences between companies and market needs, even within different divisions of the same business that influence how best to construct innovation processes.

But I found that doing this exercise again from a strategic point of view was different from the previous times I had done it from an operational standpoint. More and more I recognised that all the time we were spending focused purely on improving the process, whilst useful, was not on its own going to achieve the goals in growing the business through new products, it was just one step forward. And what I really learnt during this time, during my years based in China, in those top-down strategic roles, was that good innovation management requires not only a set of tools and techniques, but also a wide range of personal skills that need to be brought into action, before you have any chance of getting it right.

After around 25 years into my career journey, I finally appreciated that many of the skills and techniques you learn along the way, that are needed to make success of innovation and new product development in any business are not just the technical ones, not just the mechanics of the innovation processes, that absorb so much of the focus. Learning how to navigate and work with different organisational structures, particularly at the functional interfaces, and learning how to work within and shape the culture of a business, and to recognise and work with different types of people to get the best out of them, are a broad set of high level management and leadership skills that are applicable to many aspects of doing business, not just for being a good innovation manager. Early in your career, as you slowly learn about the full process of the innovation funnel, in parallel, your management skills improve. You put in better and more sophisticated processes, you might put in a more refined phase-gate process, or an Agile project management system, or new software to manage ideation, and this all helps, but it doesn't get you all the way. Your skills and your process get more sophisticated, but still you find this doesn't automatically deliver success. You might be getting better at new product development, but projects still take too long, why? And this is when you learn there are other forces at play, other factors in a business that influence the success of your ability to grow through new products: organisation and culture.

If you think back to all the political and people challenges you endured during your career, all the negotiations you had to have, all the arguments you had to try to work through, though at times incredibly frustrating, you eventually come to realise that these all contribute to building up the non-technical set of skills you need to actually make innovation happen in your business.

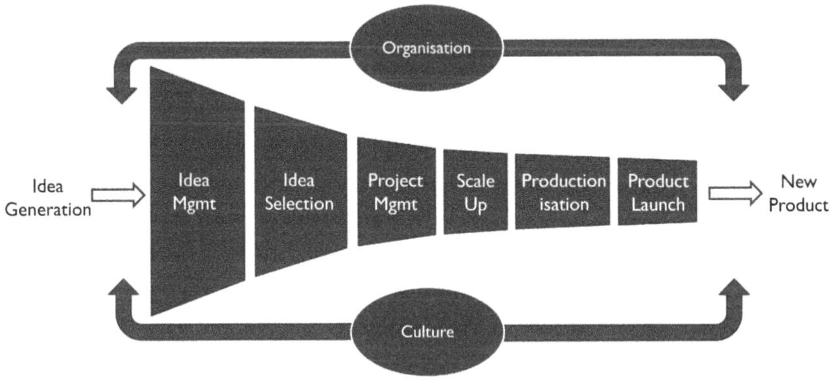

My own career path, and the associated evolution of my own experience and management skills, is of course unique, everyone has their own path. But if you are reading this book, it is very likely that is because you have, or have had at some time in your career, responsibility for technology leadership in a business. And so I suspect that, whilst your own specific path is different, you can relate pretty well to the steps along the innovation journey that unfolded before me slowly over the years. It doesn't matter what industry you are in, it doesn't matter what technology you deal with or what products you make, the longer your working life, the more career highs and lows you will experience, the more good and bad working environments you will find yourself in, and the wider the set of behaviours and people politics you will become exposed to. All of it enriching your own skills, growing your maturity as a business person and enhancing your capability to handle the ever new and diverse situations that life and business throw at you. And so, depending on where you are along your own innovation journey, some of what I describe will be very familiar, and some of it you are yet to discover yourself. In which case, I hope this narrative prepares you somewhat for what is in store and hopefully shortcuts both your journey and your own learning curve.

These days, there are plenty of courses that teach you the mechanics of how to do innovation. You can be exposed early on in your career to the concept of the innovation funnel and to all the mechanics of the innovation process. And as stated earlier, there are now plenty of companies falling over themselves to sell you "their" version of the process. Some of the courses even touch on the influence of organisation and of culture. But it is one thing to have this explained to you in a short course, it is another thing entirely to live and breathe it over many years, with every step a learning experience and with the whole thing unfolding out slowly before you as you progress in your career through business. When I started out on this journey 30 years ago, there were very few people, if any, who understood this holistic picture. The business world was still trying to find its way through building an effective set of business processes to try to manage the apparent chaos of innovation within a business. It is only now, that enough of us have been through this journey that we can begin to educate the next generation on not only how it works, but also, how to actually do it. That is why I am so keen to make sure that my books do not offer just a textbook approach to innovation, but actually provide real world counsel on how to apply it in different situations and in different types of businesses. Because one thing I have learnt time and time again on my innovation journey, is that no matter how many times we try to reinvent, recreate or improve on a business process, be it project management documentation, be it waterfall or Agile, be it idea management techniques, there is no one-size-fits-all solution. Every business is different, every market has different dynamics, every team of people behave and interact in unique ways, and so there is no real substitute for experience when it comes to effective application of techniques to manage innovation.

The Business Innovation Maturity Journey

In summarising the career long personal experiences in this chapter that make up my own innovation journey, and in finally reaching an understanding of what was happening around me in the businesses within which I worked and the many others I worked with, and observing how these organisations as a whole evolved on their own innovation journey, it helped me to develop a simple model to map out the "innovation maturity journey" that any business travels down, depicted below.

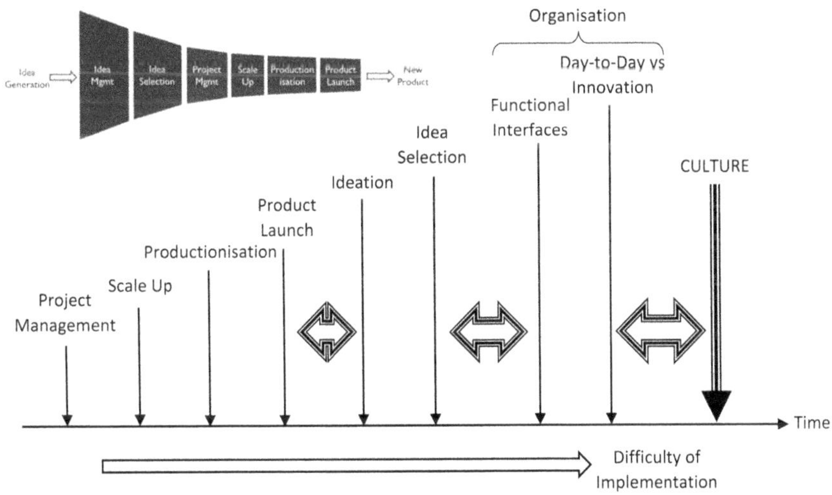

Once a business takes the decision to improve its ability to grow through new products, whether it's a decision taken right at the top by the CEO or board, or locally by the individual leading new product development, the first step taken is always to tighten up their project management skills and processes. This forms the first step down the innovation funnel, albeit one in the middle of the funnel. Project management is a fundamental skill that needs to be present in any new business and new product development programme. Without it, any business will struggle to deliver such activities on time and on budget. At some point along the maturity journey, a business will also wake up to having to develop portfolio management skills as well, as it realises trying to juggle multiple projects requires a different, and additional, set of tools and disciplines, though this is not central to the maturity journey and tends to happen either at the same time as the project management step or in parallel, alongside the first few steps.

As I described in the story of my own innovation journey earlier in this chapter, a business then quickly moves through the next steps of scale-up, productionisation and product launch, usually as it expands its project management process into a broader phase-gate mechanism, covering all of the key steps required in the holistic project management of new product development projects to full commercialisation. These steps can be introduced all at the same time, but invariably a business doesn't fully address each step in detail until projects they are currently working on progress into those stages themselves.

Once a business has fully implemented the first four steps and embedded the appropriate tools, techniques and disciplines within the organisation, it now feels like it is in better control of delivering its new product development projects, so it has reached an important milestone along its innovation maturity journey. At this point, in my experience, a business then starts to look back up the innovation funnel and starts to think about how it can better select better quality projects to work on, with better return and better chance of succeeding and then back further, on how it can better generate and capture ideas in the first place. This leads the business to creating mechanisms to select the best ideas, and ultimately to the whole business of ideation. A business can then typically get carried away at this point with idea generation techniques, bringing in ideation experts to get people thinking in a different way, and organising ideation events, and starts talking about "blue skies", "three-box strategy', "blue ocean strategy" or other innovation industry buzzwords and phrases they have heard about, and thinking that these will be the answer to all the company's prayers on finding a new direction for the business, an earth-shattering new product or lucrative new market place. Good luck with that. It's certainly possible and a vital starting point, but often, even in the case of such endeavours generating some potentially exciting ideas, at this point along their innovation maturity journey, a business is rarely mature enough both organisationally and culturally to take these ideas forward. Once the harsh realities of the next quarterly financials hit the leadership team, all those great ideas usually get swept to one side and forgotten about, without having had more than a quick look see, in a token gesture that something should be done with the workshop outputs. Sad but true.

At this stage, the innovation funnel is essentially complete, and many of those senior leaders responsible in a business for innovation and new product development believe that they have got their innovation process locked down and working well, and are starting to feel pretty pleased with themselves. A business will then typically go through a honeymoon period, sometimes for several years, putting ideas and projects through their processes reasonably diligently, and every two or three years dusting the processes down, doing some maintenance, or sometimes a major overhaul (especially if there is a new boss in charge of the whole process, which over a three-year period is often the case). Too many businesses sit languishing at this stage on their innovation maturity journey and never realise that their journey is not complete. This point is the first truly major hurdle, and requires not just a next step, but a huge leap, to progress to the next stage. To leap this chasm, it is first necessary to develop the wisdom to understand that just having an innovation process, a well-oiled machine though it might be by then, is still not the final answer to growth through new products. Unfortunately, it will usually take several years for a business to figure this out in isolation, without the benefit of external advice. Eventually someone should notice because the financial performance reports should be giving them sufficient feedback, especially the underperforming percentage of new product sales trends and any other innovation-related KPIs. It takes several years because the typical response to underperforming trends is to replace the person in charge of innovation, and the new person invariably wants to reinvent the wheel and put in a new innovation process, because the last one obviously wasn't working. Well, guess what. If all you do is replace the innovation process with another innovation process, this is unlikely to move the needle that much, because the business has not yet realised what's missing from the picture and has yet to take the next big leap across to reorganising its structure to better handle the shared responsibilities, clear accountabilities and smooth project handovers that an innovation organisation really needs to become more effective. This type of reinventing the wheel can unfortunately go through several cycles before someone is strategically minded or experienced enough to recognise the true nature of the problem, namely the fact that the organisation and culture of the business are the real barriers to innovation and to growing the business through new products.

Once a company decides to make the leap to an organisation that supports innovation rather than hinders it, by taking into account the need to manage its key functional interfaces and to morph into a more collaborative structure, it soon discovers that this big change is only step one, and that the duality of the business in terms of the need to have both an effective day-to-day and an efficient innovation organisation at the same time is a significant business transformation challenge (we will explore this in more depth in Chapter 5). Passing through this stage involves the biggest trauma that the business is ever likely to have to handle internally and requires a bold, practical and well-managed plan, plus a lot of patience, to handle all the people issues that major structural transformations inevitably create and have to deal with to avoid self-destruction.

Once the pain of transformation is over, and it will surely be painful for some, the business should start to see new product delivery becoming more effective, though probably still not achieving the stretch goals that the business really aspires to achieve. This is where the final push is required. This is where ultimately and inevitably a business has to turn its focus on to the biggest challenge of all and the fundamental hindrance to delivering effective innovation; people, their behaviours and attitudes and the business culture that that creates. The leap from transforming into an effective organisation and getting the individuals within that organisation to collaborate effectively and openly together is the biggest chasm of all along the journey. The right organisation has to come first, because the behaviour of people within any organisation is not only a consequence of their own personalities and how they interact with others, their behaviours are modified by the boundaries within which they have to act, and this is organisation, this is reporting structures, incentive schemes and KPIs. That is why organisational reform has to come first, because otherwise, any cultural change that is implemented may not happen in the right way and to the right end.

One thing you should take note of on the model is that the x-axis is time, to indicate progress through the innovation maturity journey, but also, alongside the progress over time, there is also an increasing degree of "difficulty of implementation" of all the steps. This is not because to progress through each of the later steps requires any more clever thinking than the previous ones, or that the tools and techniques that you have to create and implement get any more complex, it is simply that as you progress from one step to the next, you have to involve more people, get their buy-in and involvement, and that is the most difficult thing of all. And in my experience, this difficulty is not linear through the journey, it is closer to being exponential.

By the time you have a complete innovation funnel in place in your business, with the full set of tools and techniques that requires, you will have roped in most of the key heads of departments into your form filling requirements and into regular meetings, which will have been a major achievement in itself. But to step forward into making the necessary organisational changes and then on ultimately to make the cultural changes that need to be addressed, this requires you and your innovation programme to touch every single person in an organisation, which depending on the size, scale and complexity of your business, can be a truly momentous task. This is why companies rarely get beyond just setting up a set of innovation processes, rarely get into making the structural changes necessary and extremely rarely get to develop the culture needed to build their business into one that is truly capable of growing effectively through new products and innovation. And the other key reason it takes so much time and increases in difficulty over that time, is that if the evolution takes many years and sometimes decades to occur naturally, then there will have been several changes to leadership and other key personnel along the way, each of which brings new points of view to accommodate and new behaviours to deal with. Any long-term programme of evolution and change has to be fluid, because you will naturally be dealing with a slowly changing business, both internally and externally, as you always need to keep your organisation market focused.

This model displays in a simple way the hierarchy of steps that any business naturally goes through, and needs to go through, in order to get to a truly efficient innovation focused business. Even if you are aware of the whole journey and all of its steps right from the start, you cannot get there in one leap, you have to focus on each step and make that work before you have the tools and mindset to move on to the next. Every organisation has to lay the right foundations. Not every business has to, or will, follow exactly the same order of steps, they can do some of the early ones in a different order, or merge a couple of the steps together, but in my own experience the model summarises what I have observed happen over many years in many businesses as they mature.

If left unmanaged, this innovation maturity journey can take established businesses decades to travel, suffering long painful years of small incremental refinements, failed experiments, brief victories, and leadership churn. But it doesn't have to be that way. The whole process can be shortcut and decades of evolution can be reduced to two or three years of targeted and appropriately resourced activities. This is what this book is all about, so read on.

To close this chapter, I want to return to the critical importance of leadership in making innovation successful in any business because time and time again I have observed how successful growth through new products starts at the top.

Why Do Businesses Struggle to Grow through New Products? It All Starts at the Top

I've worked for too many businesses that said they were entrepreneurial and weren't, that said that they were collaborative and weren't, that said that they wanted to grow by developing new products but struggled to deliver. But why? I'm sure the leadership meant well, I'm sure they wanted these things, but why didn't they happen?

Over time, it became clear to those of us working in these businesses that such proclamations were all just words in a mission statement, or part of a CEO's high-level speech, and that they never actually transformed into real, practical action. I'm sure in every case the CEO and the executive team wanted to have all these things in their business, but why didn't they get them? What stopped them? What I learnt as I moved up the corporate ladder and progressed into the C-suite myself, was one of the things that stopped them was that their organisations were not actually set up to be entrepreneurial, or to collaborate or to develop and deliver new products. Experience has taught me that when business leaders announce such things, there is too often a tendency for them to just sit back and expect that the business would just get on and do them (they didn't), and that delivering these things was someone else's job. The boss has done their job, haven't they? He or she has said what they want, surely that's enough?

Fortunately, my own experience of such things is not universally repeated in every business, and there are examples of company CEOs getting it right. My good friend and part time collaborator, Cliff Spiro, worked at GE during the golden days, under CEO Jack Welch. Cliff spent 21 years in GE in R&D and general management roles, before moving on to even more senior technology management roles at other companies. During Jack Welch's 20-year tenure at the top, from 1981 to 2001, he grew the business from $25 billion to $130 billion, with the share price rising from below $10 to around $60, a level it has never since returned to. There are no doubt many reasons for Jack Welch's success, many strategies he successfully employed, with plenty of them heavily documented in multiple articles and books, and taught at business management courses across the planet, but one important thing that Cliff related to me – of great relevance to this current topic – is that Jack took close personal control of his own company-wide initiatives. Every two years he would announce a new headline goal, ranging from cost reduction, to sales growth, etc., all very similar to the type of things I had experienced in businesses I had worked, but the difference in GE, was that Jack would take personal charge of each of these schemes. He would relentlessly drive them down the organisation, reviewing progress with managers at every opportunity, and monitoring results regularly throughout the two-year period until the goals were achieved. This for me sets the benchmark of how senior management should behave, announce big goals and follow them up personally – don't just abdicate responsibility to others. No one is ever going to believe in such headline announcements as much as the person at the top that initiated them.

Another example of good ownership of a companywide leadership initiative, this time in a business I actually worked in at the time, so I was part of it firsthand, was when I worked in the Thermal Products Division of Morgan Advanced Materials, a billion-dollar public limited company listed on the UK FTSE 250. The President of the Division, Ian Robb, my boss at the time, was very passionate about the wellbeing of his employees, both physically and mentally. A natural people person, Ian was the ultimate flag-waving, "rallying the troops" kind of leader. The type of person that got to know everyone and their families personally. Ian launched a company-wide "Better You Better Life" initiative which he, along with us in the leadership team, actively drove throughout the many businesses around the world in our global division. The breadth of the initiative encompassed many diverse types of well-being, healthy eating and exercise activities, some cascaded top-down, some built bottom-up from the operational sites themselves, but it also extended to plenty of other fun and frivolous activities that boosted team working and employee engagement, improving the culture of the business worldwide and making it a much more pleasant and desirable place for people to work. Although this type of initiative is not directly related to growth through new products, and is difficult to tangibly link to the business' financial performance, it is one of the best examples I have personally been involved with of how a single determined and passionate leader can transform the hearts and minds of people throughout a business, and there is much to learn from it. However, such positive examples of CEOs and other business leaders taking personal ownership of companywide initiatives that delivered tangible benefits, are in my own experience, unfortunately few and far between and certainly not the norm.

So why do businesses and business leaders regularly make these same mistakes? To state something at the top is a great and necessary start, but if you don't follow it up, don't be surprised if it doesn't actually happen. But why do organisations struggle with fostering entrepreneurial and collaborative behaviours and with developing and delivering new products? Why is it so difficult to deliver on such high-level aspirations?

One key contributor is the nature of the bosses that boards inevitably appoint into the position of running a company. Such leaders tend to be classic business management professionals, who have usually come up through the functional ranks of finance, operations or sales, sometimes with an MBA bolted on the side at some point in their career. These types of leaders have been taught how to execute the current business model, and are incentivised and focused on delivering the numbers, quarter by quarter. They typically implement a classic set of metrics, like ROCE (return on capital employed) and IRR (internal rate of return), which drives the business to squash overhead, outsource services and only justify investments that deliver short term returns. Such cycles of short-termism can deliver great profitability and highly lucrative bonuses for the top team, after which the CEO moves on to his next company leadership position to repeat this strategy. And whilst they're doing all this, as part of their town hall sessions with employees, the CEO will usually give the speech about collaboration, growing the business, developing new products. Probably all well-meaning and with the best of intent, but when they come to actually making the investment decisions needed for long term sustainable growth, they find such projects don't contribute well to their ROCE/IRR metrics, and so investment, and prioritising R&D and new product development to deliver profitable, sustainable growth, take a back seat, or worse, get cut as overheads. I have experienced this several times in my career, when I was offered big, new roles, backed up with promises of major resources to deliver on big growth goals for the business, which quickly fizzled away when it came to making the investment decisions, leaving me without the resources to deliver on what I was being employed to do. I am sure I'm not alone in this experience. This whole situation and leadership behaviour are even worse in publicly listed companies, as leadership team decisions are focused almost exclusively on trying to keep the share price high, in the belief that they are there to maximise shareholder value. The leadership behaviours that produce short-term focus are a major reason why big businesses struggle to diversify. They directly create an internally focused business, lost in its own world, with too many of their employees locked into cycles of cost down, too many internal initiatives and endless internal reporting, losing sight of the markets they serve, losing the vision to see where these markets are heading and without the resources to do anything meaningful about future trends and opportunities. Whilst these types of leadership challenge are mostly the stuff of big corporations, smaller businesses are not without their struggles.

What I have observed over my career is that as businesses grow, they undergo a natural evolutionary cycle. As a business evolves from a start-up it grows organically through sales growth of its start-up product, then eventually it will naturally get to the point that it needs to diversify as it saturates its initial market or meets strong competition. It then needs to expand and diversify its product offering to grow. It may do this through acquisition, but if it chooses to do it organically, then all the skills and strengths that made it grow from a successful start-up suddenly grind to a halt when it comes to diversification and new product development. Why? Because businesses initially develop as organisations designed to deliver the day-to-day business of doing business: make stuff – sell stuff – deliver stuff – collect money – repeat. That's how business works, that's how they are therefore organised. But innovation and new product development doesn't work like that and needs a different style of organisation to succeed.

In their first attempts in trying to diversify and create new products to grow, businesses typically try to squeeze out new products by trying to drag the process through the existing organisation by handing out "and" jobs to those good people that helped the business get where it is. Those people do their best, but they inevitably find it really hard to deliver because the mechanisms and resources to support innovation are lacking in the organisation, leading to plenty of frustration and finger-pointing all round. This is the phase where developing new products is often viewed as an "and" job because there is too much day-to-day business stuff to do. Whilst the need for new product development may be well recognised to grow the business, executing it is not an easy thing, as most businesses find out the hard way. The next phase of the evolution is that the business then hires in new people, good technical people, good business development people, and then tries again and sits back and waits again. Surely this will succeed? Maybe, but often not. These experts soon find themselves trying to work within organisations that just don't have the right business processes, have no clear chain of accountability, that lack formal handover of ownership of projects down the pipeline and that suffer from a weak (or even worse, a toxic) culture of collaboration and innovation.

The evolution of a business from a traditional "make stuff – sell stuff" structure to one that seamlessly integrates an innovation organisation delivering profitable new products successfully to market efficiently is a long and challenging one. It can take a company many painful years to achieve this. If left to evolve naturally, the transformation can take five years for some businesses, and much longer than this for bigger, more complex multinationals. The only way to shortcut this is to recognise this early on in the evolution of your business and take steps to manage the transformation rather than let it try to happen naturally.

So What Can You Do about It?

If it is your responsibility to lead a business, either as CEO or part of the board, in my 30 years in industry, I have observed that there are four key things you need to put in place right at the start if you want to lead your business down the road of transforming it into one that can develop and deliver new products effectively:

1) Authenticity – you've got to really mean it. Don't just say it, you need to follow up with action and make it happen.
2) Honesty – be self-critical about your organisation, recognise the limitations of your organisational structure and that things need to change.
3) Invest – put your money where your mouth is. Understand that reorienting your business for growth through new products requires targeted funding and is an investment like any other. Ring-fence and dedicate resources or you will never deliver what you set out to.
4) Plan – treat the transformation like a project, put in a plan, KPIs and manage and monitor progress regularly.

If you start with these four things, then you will successfully reorganise your business ready to profit and grow from new product development and you can then lead it with confidence into its next phase of growth.

3

TECHNICAL SUCCESSES, COMMERCIAL FAILURES

> It is too easy once a project is launched to put your head down and pedal like hell, only to find when you raise your head again, that the road has moved.
>
> Chris Parr, VP Science & Technology at Imerys Aluminates

When thinking about new products, many of those involved in business focus almost completely on the science, technology and engineering aspects (and most industry conferences are full of companies wanting to tell you all about their great new product technologies) because to many, it's the most exciting and interesting bit. But what people often don't think about is the entire process of innovation that has to happen within an organisation to create a new product and transform it into a commercial success. If it's been your project that you have diligently managed, your new product that you have carefully nurtured, it is very easy to get wrapped up in the excitement of your new technology – and you should. But to make it a commercial success – and after all, that's the whole point of creating new products in business – you need to be well aware of, and well prepared for, all the barriers and hurdles you will face in bringing it to market. If you want your new product to be a success, being a great technologist is no guarantee of that. You also need to develop a whole host of additional skills in order to manage your new baby through your organisation, surround yourself with a great team that can fill in the gaps in your skill set, and build the right relationships within your business to "oil the wheels" for your project.

In the previous chapter, I have described my long innovation journey, about how over many years, I learnt all about the process of innovation, and subsequently just how much that process is at the mercy of how a business is structured and of the working culture it develops. But how do you actually learn all that stuff? You learn it by doing it, by developing new products and trying to make a success of them. You learn some of it from your colleagues, some from your bosses, some from books and seminars, some from consultants and experts, and you learn some of it by doing it yourself and finding what works. But you also learn by trying things and failing. And the failures are usually the most valuable lessons of all. And the most valuable of failures that you will encounter along your innovation journey are the projects that become known as "technical successes", which is a polite way of saying a "commercial failure".

All of us who have long careers in technology and innovation will have examples of such "technical successes" in their work history, projects that seem to tick all the boxes, that have clear commercial applications, real customer pull, clever technology that works, but which for one reason or another never make any money, never live up to their potential and do not make it to commercial success. For me, these types of projects were where I really learnt about what I described in my previous book as the 3Ps: "people, politics and process", and were particularly where I began to see all the barriers to innovation that I captured in Chapter 2 of that book. But more than that, when things go wrong, you get to see just how a business works, how departments interact (or don't) and how people behave (both good and bad). And the organisation, process and culture of a business become truly exposed.

So, by way of illustration of these points, in this chapter I'm not going to tell you about my career successes, I'm going to tell you about some of my failures. I'm going to dig deep into a couple of my own "technical successes, commercial failures" to show how they expose the how and why that businesses struggle with when developing new products. I wouldn't normally discuss any details of commercial technologies I have worked on or of companies I've worked with or name individuals in any of my books, for the obvious reasons of confidentiality, liability and integrity. But in the case of the following two projects I am going to cover as examples of "technical success, commercial failures", I can talk about these particular technologies because they are all patented, and have been presented by myself, several times at international conferences in open forum, and so all the information about the technology and the products is already out there in the public domain.

Both projects ran between 15 and 20 years ago, during what I now consider to be my golden age of creativity when it comes to innovative new technologies. I had a great team, a great mixture of highly talented material scientists and practical "roll up the sleeves" doers. We all just got on with stuff and delivered a huge amount on slim resources during that time. We had some great success during that period, from which I learnt a lot about the process of "transforming technology into profit", but these two particular projects stand out to me as notable examples which achieved all their technical aims, but failed to deliver any significant return, and these in particular taught me much about what can go wrong during the long and complex process of "transforming technology into profit". My key technical collaborator during that period was a guy called Nashim Imam. Nash is one of the most energetic and passionate material scientists you could ever meet. A real powerhouse of wanting to get things done, move things forward. And a real pleasure to work with.

I will apologise up front if these next two sections get a bit too "techy" for you. But I do need to give some degree of background to explain what the two projects were all about and to provide some context. I am well aware that one of the barriers to innovation is not communicating it effectively to the audience, and I have seen first-hand how too much "technical" detail can turn off non-techies very quickly. I hope I have pitched it right, but feel free to skim through the next couple of pages and go straight to the learning points, as these form the main purpose of this chapter.

Case Study 1: Rammable Conductive Lining (RCL)

This new product development project came out of conversations I had with a large global company that manufactures induction furnaces. I had been working with them for a while on optimising the use of foundry crucibles in their induction furnaces, trying to match the material properties of the crucible with the electrical characteristics of the induction fields.

Induction furnaces are electrically powered furnaces in which the heat is applied by induction heating to a metal. This is achieved using a high voltage electrical source, in the form of a primary coil, which induces a low voltage, high current in the metal (or in a secondary coil), which heats up the metal. Induction heating is essentially a way of transforming electrical energy into heat energy. Induction furnaces are typically used to melt iron and steel, copper, aluminium and precious metals, and range in capacity from small units melting under a kilogramme up to those handling a hundred tonnes. Induction furnaces are generally used in foundries to produce alloys, but also by other industries for heat treatment of metals, or in coating and galvanizing operations. Different metals couple with the induction field of the primary coil to different extents, such that some metals work much better with induction heating than others, primarily ferrous metals. For example, with aluminium, coupling is poor, and one way to get around that is to use a furnace lining material which couples well with the field inside the coil and heats up just like a metal. As the lining material is in contact with the aluminium, heat transfer occurs by conduction from the lining to the aluminium, thus heating up the metal indirectly. This is where electrically conducting high temperature materials like carbon, graphite and silicon carbide are useful, and these form the basis for such lining materials. A crucible made of graphite (a crystalline form of carbon) and silicon carbide can be made that fits inside an induction furnace coil, and a charge of aluminium alloy placed inside. In this way, induction furnaces can be used to melt alloys that don't naturally couple with induction fields.

One practical challenge of using indirect heating with a furnace liner is that the pre-formed crucibles that are used for the liners can be very large – over 2 m high and 1.5 m wide in some cases – making handling and furnace refit a big job. And because they are preformed items, they come in limited sizes and geometries, with induction furnaces having to be designed especially around them. During my ongoing meetings with the senior staff of the induction furnace manufacturer, there was one comment from their president that piqued my interest: "it would be great to have a lining material that we could install *in situ* in the furnace, which was not constrained by size or geometry". For our customer, the induction furnace manufacturer, such a product could allow them to produce much larger furnaces for aluminium and extend their technology into other non-ferrous applications, growing their addressed market and gaining a real advantage against their competitors. For us, as the manufacturer of the lining materials, such a product could massively increase the types of induction furnace we could sell to, increasing considerably our market potential in this sector, moving us out of the small-scale foundry environment into the much larger primary aluminium sector. It seemed a real win-win opportunity. But to create such a product from the existing state of the art seemed a massive technical challenge. There were some significant technical hurdles to overcome:

1) The existing lining materials based on graphite and silicon carbide were made by compacting a mixture of these materials with binders and additives at high pressure, using techniques such as roller forming or isostatic pressing, and then firing at high temperature to form a carbon-bonded product. The pre-formed mixture was certainly mouldable and might well form the basis of a new *in situ* lining material, but in the pre-formed, unfired state the material was not electrically conductive, as the binders were solvent-based, and so could not couple with the induction field once installed in a furnace.
2) Carbon- and graphite-based products are susceptible to oxidation when used at temperatures above 300° C, and so the existing pre-formed and pre-fired crucible lining products are protected with a surface coating of glaze to stop oxygen in the air attacking the carbon in the products during use. Since the heat treatment and melting of metals in induction furnaces reaches temperatures well above 300° C (typically 700–1400 °C depending on the metal), if we installed carbon and graphite containing materials *in situ* into a furnace, how are we going to stop the oxidation during use? Any such lining would just burn away once heated up.
3) Since the mouldable pre-formed mixture used binders that were solvent-based, if we installed it *in situ* and found some way to heat it up to fire it ready for use, then the solvent would immediately decompose and vaporise into hydrocarbon gases, and we would be filling up the workplace with clouds of noxious smoke. Not a user-friendly product at all. It would be immediately banned on health and safety grounds.

Not to be deterred, and given the significant potential this opportunity presented to expand this market sector for us, we prepared a set of technical, practical and performance targets for the product and went through a series of brainstorming sessions (some more formal, and some chatting over a coffee) to determine if we had a chance of overcoming these technical hurdles, using our existing materials technology as a starting point. I have to say, I was immensely proud of the technical team and how we worked together for this project. The brainstorming sessions were very creative and generated some awe-inspiring potential solutions to the problems. Once we had selected a few technologies to throw at the problem and worked up a plan, the team worked systematically, kept well to deadlines and in the end, really delivered. The team stepped up and worked through each problem one by one. The solutions we arrived at, and the development programme that ensued, became the basis of the patents, "Methods of making inductively heatable articles, induction furnaces and components, and materials" (EP1588386, GB2393500A, CN100418922C) but in summary, the novel solutions that we employed are described as follows:

1) To solve problem one – the fact that the unfired material mix was non-conductive electrically and so would not couple with the furnace induction field in a furnace – we set about incorporating a variety of materials and additives that would increase the connectedness between the particles. In simple terms, the more the conductive components in the mix are touching each other, the more electricity can be conducted once installed in a furnace. So we sought out materials that would promote particles to touch each other as much as possible. It was then a question of could we incorporate enough of such particles into the mix to achieve sufficient conductivity to couple with the induction field. Fortunately, by using the following blend of additives we achieved this:
   a. Carbon fibres – distributing very fine in diameter, high-aspect-ratio carbon fibres throughout the mix achieved a huge number of physical connections as the fibres bridge particles. As carbon is electrically conductive, then this additive increases the conductivity of the bulk mix. Carbon fibres are a relatively expensive additive, but you only need a very small percentage to achieve the inter-connectedness between particles we were

looking for. Today, you could probably do the same thing with graphene, but this project was running ten years prior to the isolation and characterisation of graphene.

b. Exfoliated graphite – graphite is a crystalline form of carbon, in the form of flakes, where the crystals are composed of layers. By heat treating the graphite flakes very quickly, and to a very high temperature, it makes the layers expand, creating a concertina-like appearance in the flakes/crystals. Using this as an additive in the mix, as part replacement for standard graphite flakes, increases the number of touch points between particles, thus increasing electrical conductivity.

2) To solve problem two, the problem that the unfired material mix was susceptible to catastrophic oxidation once heated above 300° C, we knew we could not apply a glaze onto the lining installed *in situ* – it just wasn't practical. A glaze is essentially a complex mixture of glasses, designed to melt slightly across the range of use temperatures to form a physical barrier to prevent oxygen getting through. To solve this problem, we used our deep knowledge of glass-forming chemistry and some quite sophisticated computer modelling techniques to design a tailored glass chemistry, which on heating would form a glass composition to produce self-glazing behaviour during use. Simply put, we put the glaze inside the mix, instead of on the surface, a real ground-breaking concept in the industry – and it worked.

3) To solve problem three – the potential for the product to produce clouds of noxious fumes on heat up – we replaced the solvent-based binder systems with a novel water-based suspension of ultra-fine carbon particles (called colloidal carbon). Not really a binder in the normal sense of the word, these colloidal carbon type products were normally used as lubricants designed to assist manufacture in the metal forging industry. This ensured only water would be released during heat up as steam, and the extra carbon contributed to the conductivity of the bulk product on initial heat up.

The new product we ended up creating had a lot of positives going for it. It was a completely new concept in materials technology for induction heating systems. RCL had the capability to open up new applications, which were previously impossible with current induction heating systems and materials, and could extend the working temperature of existing applications. It was an *in situ* rammable, conductive carbon/ceramic lining material that could couple with the induction field in the unfired state, such that it could be fired *in situ* without emission of noxious fumes, without the need to pre-condition the lining, without thermal shock issues and without degradation of the lining during use through oxidation.

For commercialisation, we named the product RCL, after rammable conductive lining. RCL was truly innovative. Its behaviour is still unique amongst unfired carbon and ceramic products, as the electrical resistivity of such systems is normally much too high to couple with induction fields at normal frequencies, even 15 years on. The project team's creative programme of materials development overcame these limitations to create a complex functional materials technology that could couple with standard frequency induction fields in the unfired state. The original focus of the material/system development was the metal melting/foundry sector, but it quickly became apparent that the material and concept would have practical uses in other applications. We did a lot of trials, both in-house and at several customers around the world. Work with several major induction heating equipment manufacturers demonstrated the practical benefits of the material in metal melting, incineration and glass melting applications, as well as other applications where localised temperature control in high temperature operations was a benefit, such as metal billet and wire heaters and non-conducting rammed linings in induction furnaces. I remember one trial in particular, in Norway, where the material was being used as an inductively heated source to ignite waste diesel, for a novel on-board incinerator system in shipping, designed to comply with new waste emissions regulations. Seeing those flames shoot out of the end of a cylinder of our material was an exciting and new experience for us. It looked like we had invented a new type of flamethrower.

The practical benefits of RCL were numerous. This new material concept and the unique abilities of RCL allowed faster turnaround when relining the induction system. In addition, since the electrical characteristics of the unfired RCL were similar to the fired material, areas of the lining that were showing signs of wear could be repaired, thus extending greatly the time between full relines. Since RCL was placed *in situ*, it offered the induction system designer the ability to optimise coil design without the constraints of lining shape or geometry. This meant that designers for molten metal handling were no longer constrained to an existing pre-formed crucible shape.

It really was a great technical success, and one that I count amongst the best and most creative that I was involved with in my career – certainly in my top ten projects. So imagine my surprise and frustration when RCL did not go on to become a great commercial success. Despite so many positive trials, and so much interest amongst the customers we exposed it to, we ended up selling very little. And as the sales dwindled early on, the light quickly fizzled out as everyone moved on to other projects and attention became diverted elsewhere.

RCL – Key Learning Points

So what went wrong? Why did such a clever, highly innovative technology not achieve commercial success? As a project it went through all the classic innovation funnel steps, it had good project management, it had commercial pull, it had a good technical team working on it, it went through lots of successful trials in a number of different and diverse applications and there was interest from a number of potential customers. So why did it fail commercially? I personally presented the product at several international conferences: in Turkey, India, across Europe and the USA. Why did it not take off in the market?

When you're working in a busy company, with a full workload on your desk every day, it is very difficult to find the time to sit back and analyse everything that goes wrong, especially as a team, even though you know doing so could be very valuable. Some projects succeed, some fail, many hover somewhere in between and become partial successes. This is where having a robust innovation process adds value, particularly a phase-gate style approach and solid portfolio management. Not proceeding through a formal review of the RCL project at the end allowed the weaknesses in our systems to linger. At this stage of my career, and with the resources at our disposal, our rollout of such processes was not sufficient to force such a review. Some lines of communication had perhaps broken down, and RCL was not of course the only new product development project we were working on as a team and as a business – we had several projects on the go. Like in many businesses, our team resources were stretched thin, but any business needs to maximise the use of its assets, so that was fine, that's the real world. Our portfolio management was quite good, but there was a natural tendency to focus on things that were going forward well, rather than stop and spend time reviewing those things that hadn't gone so well. It takes a degree of maturity to get a team to refocus on its failings in order to extract the positives from the situation.

One thing I learnt during this project was just how critical teamworking across different business functions is. The teamworking within the technical team was superb, and really delivered, but the team work and communication between the technical team and the sales team was by comparison quite poor. I guess this indicated, to some degree, a silo organisation. Even though we had good personal relationships between the individuals concerned, on a professional level there must have been something in the attitudes of some of the people involved on both sides which was coming between us when it came to delivering this particular project.

Another problem that I can see in hindsight is although there was top management involvement in project portfolio reviews, evidenced by the good depth of debate we had at quarterly executive meetings, ultimately, the actual portfolio of projects that we worked on was really up to my discretion. There wasn't a lot of input on deciding which new products to focus on. There was plenty of discussion on projects during their progress, which was great, but not so much on choosing the projects in the first place. I think partly this was because the executive team generally trusted me as the technical expert (nice to know), partly because some of them were bored by the whole technical arena and did not feel they could, or didn't want to, contribute too much (a shame). The overall problem with this way of managing the portfolio of projects was that there was no real involvement of the top team in shaping what new product development projects we should be working on as a business, it was all left down to me and my own judgement to decide, and so RCL became something of a personal crusade for me: my pet project. Portfolio reviews at board meetings were essentially reactive, not proactive, and discussions tended to either reinforce the direction we were heading in, or be overly critical when someone didn't like a particular project. But no one on the board at that time ever suggested a new project, or a new market, or a new product we should be considering, which in hindsight reinforced for me the view amongst that particular senior team that they all thought new product development was something the technical director should be responsible for alone. I assumed at the time that that was normal and appropriate. It was only later in my career that I discovered that this was not the best way to manage innovation in a business.

This attitude of the technical director being solely responsible for delivering the new products was one that also permeated throughout the whole organisation. For the sales team, new product development was considered to be something the technical department did, so market and product management was left to me to lead, and the sales team would generally follow, which in hindsight was a mistake (I was still only halfway through my innovation journey at this point in my career). So one of the reasons for RCL's commercial failure was that it was never championed by the commercial team. They never owned it at all during the process of commercialisation – it was all down to me and my team. This was all indicative of a barrier in our innovation organisation, but also highlighted a failing in our processes, because there was no formal process of project handover to a commercial lead to guide the new product to commercial success. So it all stayed within the technical department, which was as much my fault as anyone else's.

The new product was never really "sold" to the sales team to get them on board, so there was no involvement or belief by the sales team. I discovered in one conversation, the hard way, that the sales manager did not believe in it. He actually said to me at one point when I was discussing organising a customer trial with him, "Well, it just doesn't work"! How stunned was I! Were we talking about the same product? The same product that had already had several in-house and customer trials? Sure, it was still a bit rough around the edges, it still needed a few practical tweaks before commercialisation, but fundamentally we had demonstrated that it "worked", that it did what we set out to do. I was at a loss to understand how our sales manager, a guy I respected, I liked working with and enjoyed a good relationship with as a friend, could possibly say "it doesn't work" to me. It was a pivotal learning moment for me. I knew that what we were working on was a real leap forward in terms of product concepts for the industry, and I knew that it was a massive technical challenge, but I was confident we had something worth moving forward with. In discussing the situation with him, I was left with the impression that RCL really was just too left-field, too different a new product, too much of a departure from how we and the industry did things at the time, too obscure for him to get his head around the concept. It really was ahead of its time and too "techy". In hindsight, I feel maybe we revelled too much in the cleverness of solving the technical issues and that it was seen as my personal pet project. It appeared that the sales manager had gone along for the ride up to a point, but enough was enough for him, and at that point it was going to be incredibly difficult to win him over. It didn't seem to matter how much technical data I showed him, it didn't matter the reports on product performance I was presenting at conferences, he had made his mind up, and that created a massive barrier to commercialisation. From that point on, it was very difficult to get sales support to spread the word amongst our customer base and do more customer trials.

These events all taught me that teamwork is vital, but not just within your own team (those that report in to you); you also need to consider the wider team, those key people you need to bring on your side to make the project successful. Managing sideways and upwards, not just downwards, are critical skills in "transforming technology into profit".

Another mistake that was made in hindsight in the RCL project, was that whilst we were busy developing the technology to create the new product, I never took the time to check in with the original customer that requested it. We did not keep in regular enough contact with them during the early phases of the project. Sure, I had listened to what they wanted, but we essentially went away and set up our project and did all our feasibility work in isolation. We did not go back and mention to the customer we were formally working on it, not until we had a working prototype to trial. I was personally looking forward to basking in the glory of the "ta-da!" moment when I got to tell the customer: "You know that new technology you asked for a while back? Well we have done it!" I wanted to revel in the big reveal. The learning point – there is not much room for ego in business. And the reality of this mistake was that when we eventually did go back to the same customer and told them that we had a working prototype, they were not that interested anymore, their thinking had moved on in the intervening 18 months. They were willing to have a go and do some trials at their premises, which had some interesting and positive results, but they were just not interested in taking it forward to bigger trials. Learning point – keep your customer involved from the start, as they will have a vested interest in making it a success, and they can tell you early on if they want to back out before you commit too much resource to the project.

One underlying challenge that worked against the success of this project was also my feeling at the time that this was my baby, something so new and exciting, and such a breakthrough technologically, that I found myself keeping things too close to my chest (which is one reason we had problems with the original customer and in working with the sales team) and in hindsight, I probably arrogantly wanted to make it a success, so I could bathe in the glory. Something which I certainly got to do with other projects and other successful new product launches, but with RCL it was not to be.

Was all of this all my fault? It was my job to deliver the new products, so I certainly feel responsible. But of course, the project was a team effort, business is always a team effort. And whilst I couldn't see it at the time, in hindsight, and after many years and many other roles in other businesses, I can now see how the structure of the organisation was working against me, and how, whilst the innovation culture was reasonably good, with generally good relationships between people and departments in the business, it had not matured enough to a stage where cross-functional interfaces were appreciated and managed effectively.

If RCL was not sales led, if the commercial viability was unproven, then why did we patent this technology? Was it the right thing to do? Partly it was politics, as there was a big push by the then CTO of the group to be more innovative and publish more patents. Unfortunately, this policy was being pushed through without any real assessment of the value to the company of what we were patenting. A classic mistake by some big companies, who measure their level of innovation by how many patents they publish. Sure, it's a tangible and easy thing to measure, but these are businesses, and as I explained in my previous book, a patent is a commercial tool, not a measure of how innovative a company is. So were we right to patent? Possibly, because the product was supplied unformed and unfired, it was a technology that could be freely reverse engineered, so there was a real risk of a competitor taking it apart and learning its secrets, so there was risk of technology loss.

However, despite the story of "technical success, commercial failure", RCL was by no means a dismal failure. Sure, it did not in itself produce a direct return on investment. The resources the company had committed to developing RCL (all the technician and management time, all the material and consumable costs, all the customer trial and travel costs) did not pay back with direct RCL sales, but there were a number of spin-off benefits that did ultimately lead to other successful products, other indirect returns. The complexity and unique technical challenge that the RCL opportunity presented us with led us into exploring a whole series of technical advancements, any one of which was a considerable step forward in the technology of our business at the time. We were presented with an exceptional opportunity that forced us to combine several of these new technologies in order to achieve technical performance, but each of the individual technologies ultimately found their way into other projects, and found themselves commercialised as part of other products in the business over the next few years.

The RCL project was an incredibly rich time of technical creativity and innovation for our team, and one thing it taught me was that sometimes, you just have to play with the technology, dance around at the edges of what might be possible. If you don't, you will inevitably stay within the boundaries of what is, of what everyone considers the current state of play. It is only by setting grand goals (like developing RCL), that push you into grand thinking and into following truly original paths. But justifying such playtime within a business is rarely going to fly. A business needs to minimise its risk of investment, it wants to place its bets on surefire returns. Paying for skunk works is usually only for mega-corporations with deep, deep pockets. And so sometimes, in smaller business, you have to dress this up within a real, commercially justified project. You have to seek out commercial opportunities that will allow you some freedom to dabble, and RCL was the ultimate in such opportunities in my career. No other project I have worked on has produced so many new and novel spin-off technologies that found their way into other products, which became solutions to other technical problems and commercial opportunities, and produced so much value for the business down the road.

What I have seen over the intervening years is that the more and more we overlay structure and rigour onto chasing new business opportunities, the more we stifle this kind of freethinking and technology playtime. Sometimes we have to fail with new technologies to open up new pathways and new possibilities. You need to give creative people room to be creative. Finding the balance within business processes to accept and manage this is a key challenge of any innovation process.

Case Study 2: Non-Oxide Bond (NOBOND)

Even before the RCL experience, much earlier in my career, I worked on a project called "Non-Oxide Bond" (NOBOND), around 20 years ago. The aim was to explore new bonding phase options in foundry crucibles, to look for new chemistries that could enhance performance compared to the then current carbon and ceramic bonded products. We had already proved and successfully commercialised hybrid bonding systems that increase service life and a whole host of performance criteria by refining the chemistry to develop other non-oxide phases in the bonds, and we felt sure that we could drive this trend further to competitive and commercial advantage. As explained in the previous section, foundry crucibles are made from graphite and silicon carbide with a few special additives, all bonded together with carbon or ceramic-based binders, pressed at high pressure, glazed and fired at high temperatures. These consumable products are used in foundries the world over to melt and hold ferrous and non-ferrous alloys in the production of cast metal components, such as car engine components and alloy wheels. For me, the secret to a major step forward in the performance of foundry crucibles lay in the binder chemistry, the glue that holds everything together. The bonding phase is often the weak link in any material, and essentially a means of getting the materials you really want, in this case graphite and silicon carbide, into a usable form.

An additional challenge with the carbon-based binders used in crucible manufacturing was that all of the types of binders used, including phenolic resins, tars and pitches, all contained VOCs (volatile organic compounds) making them unpleasant and potentially hazardous to handle and use. And the use of such materials was, and still is, coming under ever-increasing pressure due to environmental and health and safety concerns. Even today, the legislation associated with such concerns has the potential to make the use of such materials uneconomical in the next ten years due to the associated additional costs of handling. So NOBOND was very much a strategic project, designed to prepare the business for the anticipated future constraints of working with current binder materials, including even the potential risk of an all-out ban, to safeguard the future of the company.

As with RCL, the technical challenge was significant, but in the case of NOBOND, more focused. Many of the same people were involved that later worked on the RCL challenge, and NOBOND was where much of the team did their forming, and as one of the first really big technical challenges, one of the first real opportunities to put our innovation thinking caps on. The idea generation phase to develop potential solutions was hugely creative, with a number of really left-field concepts and ideas thrown into the pot. I won't bore you with the technical details too much this time, but the solution we eventually arrived at became the basis of the patent, "Drying Ceramic Articles during Manufacture" (WO03106371).

To replace the solvent containing resin, tar and pitch binders, we developed a two-component system. We retained the carbon-containing element by replacing these binders with a high carbon content glucose syrup, a product used industrially in making beer and biscuits/cookies. The syrup is essentially 80% solid sugar dissolved in 20% water, and so has none of the potential hazards of working with a solvent-based material. This in itself was great on paper, and solved all of the legislative risks associated with the existing binders, but there was one significant practical problem. After forming of the crucible products, they are heated in an oven to crosslink and set the binder system, so that they become strong enough for handling for further downstream processing. This is no problem with the solvent-based binders, but unlike when solvents boil away during heating, water boils off all at one temperature, 100° C. This meant that all of the 20% of water in the glucose syrup binder would be released at the same time as steam, cracking the product. In the industry, this is called "explosive spalling". So we could use glucose syrup to make a crucible, but we could not process it crack-free. This is where the second component of the binder system comes in. To deal with the cracking problem, the team came up with an extremely novel approach. We searched high and low for a solution, and in playing around with a number of materials in the laboratory, we discovered an immensely useful new property of a wonderful family of materials called superabsorbents.

Superabsorbent polymers (potassium polyacrylate) are fine white powders that have the capability of absorbing up to 300 times their own weight of water. Just a very small amount added to water instantly creates a stiff gel up to 60 times the original volume of powder. Superabsorbents are used in diverse applications, including in baby nappies/diapers to absorb urine and in mortuaries to stuff dead bodies, to stop the ooze leaking out as they decompose. When I presented this explanation at one project review, one witty member of the audience exclaimed, "that's a real cradle to grave product". What we discovered was that when added to our new water-based glucose syrup binder system, the superabsorbent held on to the water chemically during heat up and instead of the water all being released at one temperature, it released the water slowly over a much wider temperature range, avoiding the explosive spalling. And because of this, we discovered that using superabsorbent as an additive in the crucible formulation allowed us to get over the cracking problem during heat treatment of the product in the oven, and produce perfect crucible products. This was an exciting discovery because it offers a far-reaching potential for the manufacture of other products in other industries where they need to heat treat water containing bodies, hence the focus of our patent.

The new two-part binder system was a tremendous technological leap forward in the industry, and not only that, it delivered a 50% cost reduction against the current solvent-based binders, a real win-win. Something for the team to be really proud of. Numerous trials in manufacturing ironed out a handful of practical challenges of working with the new binder system and the crucibles they produced, and an extensive programme of customer trials followed. All sounds great so far, very positive, but what went wrong? Why is such a great technical success a case study in a chapter about commercial failures? Why did NOBOND not achieve commercial success?

NOBOND – Key Learning Points

1) What's in a name? – Who would have thought that the name of a project is so important? In terms of effective communication, positive marketing and championing of the work, I learnt with NOBOND, just how important it is to get it right. At project set-up, the "Non-Oxide Bond" project was quickly abbreviated to NOBOND. Seems simple and straightforward enough, but in reality, for anyone not familiar with the background or objectives of the project, NOBOND puts quite a different connotation on to what we were trying to achieve. NOBOND inevitably directs people to thinking we were trying to produce a crucible without a bonding phase, i.e. "no" bond, which would be a staggering technical challenge. At some point during the project it got abbreviated even further and became NBOND, as I found that there was another project in another division of the company which was also called NOBOND. This obviously led to a little

confusion at divisional review meetings, and also, I think, diluted the uniqueness of our work and of what we were trying to achieve. So remember, internal PR is very important when you are trying to create and commercialise new technologies. Do not dismiss out of hand something that seems as trivial as the name of your project, whilst it might not be the "be all and end all" to success, it does matter.

2) A highly risk-averse culture – Swapping over manufacture from the traditional resin, tar and pitch binders to something new was always going to be a big decision. The industry had been using one form or other of such binders for the last fifty years. Over 50% of our revenue was based on this technology. What I discovered when working on implementing our new technology was that when it came down to it, all the senior management, all of whom had been interested and enthusiastic all along the way in the project, when it came to a green light decision, they just could not bring themselves to take the risk of switching over. No big change is without a few hiccups, however closely it is managed. The customer trials went mostly well, but there was the occasional bad result, but those could have been due to a myriad of other reasons, not the new binder system. And so all those doubters jumped on any little wrinkle in the technology and used it to justify not going ahead with the change of binder system in production. What this whole experience demonstrated to me was just how deeply risk-averse our business was. It talked about encouraging entrepreneurial behaviours, but the actual behaviours of the management team did not support this. Unfortunately this is all too common in business. When the stakes are high, too many people do not want to stick their neck out and take a risk, and this is a significant barrier to innovation.

3) An internally driven project – Another reason that NOBOND struggled to be implemented was that it was purely an internal project driven by strategic risk management. A perfectly good reason for a project, but when it comes to a strategic project that is changing the nature of your main product line, what's in it for your customers? The solution we found for this project not only dealt with the strategic risk but also offered significant internal cost savings, a further driver for the change. Everyone in the management team wanted these things of course, that's why they sanctioned the project in the first place, but

because of the risk-averse culture, no one wants to take the responsibility of taking such a major decision. It was the same with the commercial team: the switch would offer no advantage to their customers, the products would look the same and perform the same, so what was in it for them to manage the switch? From their point of view, they carried all of the risk and none of the reward. If the sales team aren't prepared to sell the switch to their customers, it's not going to happen.

4) Bad timing – The final nail in the coffin of NOBOND was a timing and risk management issue. The project was being implemented during a time when the factory was undergoing a major transformation. A brand-new factory, with all new production equipment and a more efficient production layout had just been constructed and the 50-year-old site, with its ancient production equipment, was in the process of being decommissioned, ready to be demolished. The whole process from planning to design to construction had taken two years. With so much upheaval on site, it was not a great time to be trying to push through a major new technology product, but the business could not just take a break from innovation for two years, otherwise we would lose our competitiveness and dominant position in the market. Our NOBOND production and customer trials were being squeezed in amongst commissioning of the new plant, and around standard production, split between the old and new site during the transition. And just like with any new technology, there were commissioning challenges with some of the new equipment. In particular, we were having big problems with the brand-new production kilns, an essential part of the production process that could make or break product quality and performance. For several months, the process engineers struggled with setting up the new kilns, and at times we were experiencing up to 70% rejects at the firing stage: a major cost to the business and a massive threat to our competitiveness. Obviously, this had a huge effect on our ability to properly test NOBOND based products. If a customer trial failed, was it due to the NOBOND technology or due to kilning problems? So it became all hands to the pump on solving the urgent kiln problems, which was absolutely the right priority, but in order to do this, all the technical and engineering resource was focused on commissioning of the new kilns, and NOBOND was

> shelved for a year. The new factory was eventually brought under control, rejects reduced to more normal levels and product quality was back on track, but getting there was a very difficult time for everyone, with much finger-pointing and blame culture. Once control was re-established, people were very reticent to change anything again for some time, as they didn't want to go through the risk again. So another year of getting back to normality was required, and by then NOBOND was two years old, and things had moved on in the business; people left, priorities changed, and NOBOND was never picked back up. The moral of this story? Don't try to make too many big changes at once.

These two case study projects occurred relatively early on in my career, and were some of the earliest projects I managed after having left the corporate R&D centre to take up a role in a manufacturing business. This was still during the first half of my innovation journey, a critical time for learning, when I had laid sufficient foundation in how innovation worked in a business, but still had a lot to learn about how people and organisations worked. Of course, there were many other projects I was involved with during those years, but these two in particular taught me much about innovation. They taught me that innovation has to exist within an existing business, that try as you might, it is incredibly difficult to try to force your project through a business without the right support, without capturing the hearts and minds of the right people. And just because you have great technology, just because you have put in a great phase-gate process or Agile project management system, such sophistication does not guarantee you success. This is when I began to appreciate that there are other forces at play, other "internal factors" in a business that influence the success of new product development activities, and when I started to see that, the biggest barrier to innovation is your own business.

The Bigger Picture and an Additional Point of View

Whilst writing this book, I had the chance to discuss the issue of "technical successes, commercial failures", and compare career notes with Chris Parr, VP Science & Technology at Imerys Aluminates. I've known Chris for a long time, and our careers have crossed paths several times over the years.

Chris has over 25 years' experience leading R&D in refractories, ceramics, abrasives and construction products, and is well-known and respected in his field. Imerys Aluminates is part of the Imerys Group, the 4.6 billion Euro-turnover French multinational company that specialises in the production and processing of industrial minerals, a truly multinational entity that operates in 50 countries with more than 18,000 employees.

I asked Chris about some of his own "technical successes, commercial failures". In his early career, he recalls projects that suffered from a disconnect between the targets set at the start of a project, and the way those targets drifted over time, for a whole variety of different reasons. As he put it to me, "It is too easy once a project is launched to put your head down and pedal like hell, only to find when you raise your head again, that the road has moved".

He recalls another project where the team developed a miraculous new product in terms of performance enhancement for their customers' products. But commercial take-up was poor because it had the side effect that it restricted their customers' ability to produce new product formulations, taking away degrees of freedom from their own formulation scientists, and limiting their ability to differentiate themselves from their competitors.

Yet another project delivered new technology with wonderful performance but proved simply too expensive for their customers, and another proved great on its own, but lost efficacy when combined with other components it had to interact with in the customers' application. Such examples highlight the importance of a deep understanding of your customers' application, both technically and commercially, and illustrates the delicate balance that is often required in introducing new technologies, as they invariably form part of sensitive combinations of materials and components, where changing one component can have a dramatic effect on another.

Every business wants their products to get locked in to their customer's process, product or supply chain, but equally customers are always wary of committing themselves strategically to one critical supplier, so it has to be a win-win situation for everyone if it is going to become a success in the market. Developing and commercialising new products is complicated further by the fact that each customer touch point requires something different. Whether you are talking to an engineer, a designer, an R&D scientist, a buyer, they are all looking for something distinctly different in the product or service you are trying to design for and sell to them.

Most industrial businesses are part of a vast supply chain, supplying a component to the next business along the chain, which becomes part of a bigger assembly or device, whether it is a chemical flow control additive for use in a concrete formulation, a metallic heating element going into a laboratory oven, or a microprocessor chip going onto an integrated circuit board. Each has an upstream chain of businesses and processes that feed into creating the product, and each has a downstream chain. At the start of the chain are the base raw material producers and at the end of the chain are the OEM (original equipment manufacturers). But wherever your business is along the chain, to develop successful, saleable new products, you need to have a deep understanding of how your product fits in with the next business/application along the chain. When it comes to the OEMs at the end of their chain, their need for customer vision is a little different as it is normally oriented towards understanding their end users and consumers. The reality of course is even more complex, and there are plenty of industrial OEM companies that are designing and supplying specialist equipment back into the supply chain to enable companies to manufacture their components, usually processing or testing equipment, e.g. plasma etching equipment used in semiconductor manufacture.

I asked Chris what he feels he has learnt from his own experiences. "Getting customers involved early in the process is critical" he says. This means a combination of getting real world marketing input as soon as possible, coupled with early customer testing to keep alignment as the project progresses and the technology develops. And having the appropriate support facilities (e.g. pilot scale plant and in-house customer testing equipment) is so important, as it makes things much easier for customers to try new things out.

He also stresses the value of knowing what to take on as a business. It's important to know your capabilities and your limitations. R&D people, especially, can be an egotistical lot, and naturally want to say "yes we can do that" whenever a tough technical task comes along, as it offers an intellectual challenge. But getting too ambitious and trying to reinvent the world are risky investments for any business. Much of the literature published these days on innovation, and most innovation conferences and courses, talk about disruption, about quantum leaps and about game-changing technologies. This kind of talk may well be appropriate to the software industry where the investment to develop and prototype products can be cheaper (and faster), but in industry, such things are big risks (with the potential of major rewards for sure), but the reality in much of industry is that new product development takes a more tightly managed approach to project selection and risk management. So industrial project portfolios are normally filled with projects that a business can handle with its known resources and expertise, as these are much more likely to deliver consistent, stepwise growth year on year. Ambition is great, but also risky.

He has also learnt to appreciate that taking a realistic approach in managing projects is vital in optimising efficiency. Context is everything and understanding the size and scale of a business is very important when designing an innovation process and the supporting business tools and management approach. If your business has 2,000 R&D people, and the innovation process requires them to hand their newly developed technologies on to a dedicated, large stand-alone scale-up team, well that requires a different approach and a different set of process management tools if your R&D team is only 20 people, and they have to do all the scale-up themselves, working directly with the production team. Chris also recalls early in his career when one of his bosses, in an effort to drive through a comprehensive and super-efficient innovation process, introduced milestone meetings which threw up long lists of onerous questions, leading the teams into months of extremely arduous data gathering, much of which proved impossible, losing the project six months going round in circles. This reminds me of Chapter 2 of my earlier work, *Transforming Technology into Profit*, where I discussed many of the barriers to innovation within an business, including that many businesses become too inwardly focused and obsessed with fine-tuning their business processes, to the extent that they can lose sight of the outside world and their own customers.

Agile vs Waterfall – Does It Really Matter?

I want to close this chapter with more of my thoughts on the eternal question of Agile versus waterfall, that I touched on in Chapter 1. Before you have to deal with the challenges of organisation and culture within a business, much of the foundation of successful new product development projects relies on having robust innovation processes in place and having the skills to use them. Therefore, choosing which processes to use is important. They need to be right for your team, right for the mechanics of the business and appropriate for the technologies and projects you are managing. Project management is central to the innovation process, and so whether you go down an Agile or waterfall route, or some other form of project management process, is going to have an influence on your delivery.

I have read endless numbers of articles about how great Agile is compared to waterfall. The authors invariably take the point of view that waterfall is old-fashioned and that Agile is a far superior, modern way of managing projects, at the same time delivering a subtle subliminal message that anyone still using a waterfall approach is a dinosaur that deserves to be wiped out when the next meteor strikes. In contrast, I have never seen any articles singing the praises of the waterfall approach to project management. Partly this may simply be due to the fact the waterfall approach has been around a long time, and Agile came along as an alternative approach to project management. But how much of this is just because something newer is more fashionable and how much is this reflecting the truth that one methodology is better than another?

I read one recent article on LinkedIn singing the praises of Agile from some professor of business management in the US, telling the story of how he was advising a business leader in a huge multinational corporation, who was having a challenge managing a large portfolio of projects across multiple teams spread around the world. The business leader had a comprehensive reporting system in place, with a quarterly review session involving all project leaders at the same time. But this guy had just too many project leaders reporting to him, and the three-month interval was just way too long between reviews, hence slowing progress. The business leader was planning to put more reporting tools in place to try to get a better handle on progress, burdening the already overloaded project leaders with more administration. The advice from the professor was that instead, he should have more frequent but shorter reviews with project leaders, talking to a different handful every week, and this way speeding up communication with the whole team. The professor justified this case study in terms of a triumph of Agile over waterfall techniques. Buy why? His suggestion just makes good business sense, and represents the kind of sensible improvement put in place by thousands of successful business professionals the world over every day. Why does he have to label it as "Agile"? How does he justify that? From the tone of the article, he clearly had a personal agenda to brand himself as a modern and progressive business adviser, which is fine, but why do this under the Agile brand, a brand that thousands of people hide behind? How does that differentiate himself from all those other Agile practitioners? Improvements to business processes like this are being implemented in companies across the world continuously, as challenges and inefficiencies emerge, and these people don't wave the Agile label around when doing it, they just get on and make improvements to their business. I am always amazed at just how many experienced, well-educated CEOs fall for this kind of nonsense. It really does demonstrate the power of marketing and having a cool brand name.

One of the problems I see which has led to confusion amongst the business community is that there is a difference between "Agile" (the brand) and "agile" (the adjective). There are plenty of businesses which talk about wanting to "becoming more agile", which is great, we should all aspire to become more responsive, more alert and quick-thinking as organisations, because that's what "agile" means. But once the word is locked into a company's vision, people inevitably interpret it as "Agile" the brand, because they see the word written into consultancy product literature and project management seminars, etc. The Agile brand is a set of tools and approaches developed within the software industry, while the adjective is a general desire to improve, and that can be achieved in lots of ways. So, when a business sets a vision of becoming more agile, the leadership needs to be more specific about exactly what that means and what it is really aspiring to achieve.

But first, let's go back to basics – what actually are waterfall and Agile? The problem right at the start with these labels is that they create more jargon, which as we have already established, can be a significant barrier to innovation. If you have never been taught what these terms mean, then it is very easy to get sucked into a company culture of talking about Agile (or agile?) without really understanding what people are talking about. I am sure lots of people read these Agile versus waterfall articles and just have a vague feeling of what Agile is, just because of what the word implies. These terms originated in the software industry, though I increasingly see the use of the word Agile starting to bleed into other industrial sectors, usually catalysed by Agile consulting companies trying to promote the virtues of their "product". These days, all software companies seem to use the language of Agile in managing product development projects. If you talk with people in these businesses their language is all "sprints" and "scrums" and such. Whilst in the rest of industry we still talk about phase-gate, rather than waterfall, which adds yet another layer of confusion and misunderstanding to the situation.

One problem I see for Agile is that it suffers a lot from too much jargon, and practitioners can get caught up in their own self-absorbed language, creating a mystique around what are essentially some simple, practical approaches to project management and new product development. The internet is littered with hilariously unintelligible management-speak titles for Agile presentations, seminars and articles. "Scrum master"? Why use silly words when perfectly good ones already exist in use in industry and in the English language.

But when you're outside of the software industry, when you hear or read the name "Agile", it sounds like it should be something great, something really worthwhile having, which raises the most relevant question in terms of this book, can Agile apply to wider industry? Are there things in the Agile approach to project management which can help and/or improve the waterfall side of business? Should we all be dropping our phase-gates and jumping onto the Agile bandwagon ourselves? To answer this, we need to dig deeper into what Agile actually is and where it came from.

Agile has evolved over several years in the software industry, but it is generally considered to have been formalised by a group of seventeen software practitioners, when they published their *Manifesto for Agile Software Development*, which reads:

> We are uncovering better ways of developing software by doing it and helping others do it. Through this work we have come to value:
>
> *Individuals and interactions* over processes and tools
> *Working software* over comprehensive documentation
> *Customer collaboration* over contract negotiation
> *Responding to change* over following a plan
>
> That is, while there is value in the items on the right, we value the items on the left more.

The 17 founders of the Agile movement took their Agile Manifesto one step further, by sharing their 12 guiding principles;

1) Customer satisfaction by early and continuous delivery of valuable software.

2) Welcome changing requirements, even in late development.
3) Deliver working software frequently (weeks rather than months).
4) Close, daily cooperation between business people and developers.
5) Projects are built around motivated individuals, who should be trusted.
6) Face-to-face conversation is the best form of communication (co-location).
7) Working software is the primary measure of progress.
8) Sustainable development, able to maintain a constant pace.
9) Continuous attention to technical excellence and good design.
10) Simplicity—the art of maximizing the amount of work not done—is essential.
11) Best architectures, requirements, and designs emerge from self-organizing teams.
12) Regularly, the team reflects on how to become more effective, and adjusts accordingly.

From my point of view, as a 30-year veteran of the manufacturing industry, the philosophy promoted by the Agile Manifesto is spot on, and there is much to be admired about the attitudes and maturity of those involved in recognising this situation in their work approach and putting it all together into a manifesto. But it does not mean to say that just because they wrote it down and gave it a name that much of these attitudes and approaches didn't already exist as part of other project management methodologies and in other industries. But what has happened over the intervening years since the publication of the Agile Manifesto, is that many people and companies have jumped on the Agile bandwagon, and used it as a banner to hoover up lots of tools and techniques that already existed, rebranding them as "Agile", and then set themselves up as Agile practitioners, advisors and consultants with a ready-made toolkit to sell. Helpful for those businesses that want or need to go down that route, but not so helpful for those businesses where the Agile approach/product may not be the optimum solution. And this goes back to the underlying theme of this book, that just by putting in a new "Agile" process to manage new product development, it is very tempting for businesses to think that the job is complete, and that they can just get on with managing their day-to-day business, safe in the knowledge that they have sorted out their innovation process and can look forward to all the growth that it is going to bring them in the coming years, when in fact, the reality is that, as I have been explaining throughout this book, the process is not the limiting factor, it's organisation and culture which are the biggest barriers. This is the danger of waving "Agile" around as a headline banner. It gives the illusion that waving an Agile magic wand will solve all of a business' innovation problems, when in fact, it cannot and will not. I can understand how and why the uninitiated might hope for that. Wouldn't it be nice if we could solve something as complex as innovation and the future growth of a business just by putting in a new project management process? Who wouldn't want to sign up for that silver bullet? Interestingly, the same mass hysteria doesn't happen with waterfall/phase-gate. Maybe because they have been around much longer and are just accepted as standards, or maybe because they don't have a snappy name, so companies that use a waterfall approach tend to see it as part of a bigger whole.

As the software industry has been using and refining Agile techniques for product development for a couple of decades now, it has naturally evolved further. One evolutionary emergence is DevOps, which is an approach a little like the technology/operations functional crossover described earlier, designed to bridge the gap more effectively when productionising new software that comes out of the Agile teams. And inevitably, Agile and waterfall are even starting to merge, as people try to extract the best of both worlds (though some diehards claim it's not possible to combine the two). Evidence of this is that there is now even an Agile phase-gate process, which combines the structure of the classic phase-gate process with the self-organised teams and short cycle iterations of the Agile process, and believe it or not, something called a "water-scrum-fall".

There is much to appreciate about the Agile approach for the industrial side of business, especially in the approach to frequent, often daily, team updates to maintain a regular heartbeat to a project, its flexible approach to process, its doctrine to use the simplest tools available, and the way in which the approach splits a project into manageable chunks to ensure real progress is being made towards the ultimate goal. But how different really is the modern waterfall/phase-gate methodology compared to Agile? Both have project charters, both use Gantt charts, both have clear team members and roles, both have flexibility and adaptability built in, both put the customer first, so what's the big difference? My experience is that those who built their career in the software industry think Agile is the best, whilst those brought up in the manufacturing industry think their phase-gate approach is the best. In reality, there are already many common approaches and principles between how new product development is done in the software industry and in broader industrial manufacturing companies. But there are a couple of fundamental differences between the industries when it comes to how new product development is done in the industrial world that limits how industry might take advantage of applying Agile/DevOps. The first is due to the fact that developers in the software industry can simply sit in front of their laptop and start writing code to create their product. In the "real" world of industry, products are made from real, physical items, which have to be physically created in a laboratory or engineering workshop, assembled, scaled up for production, etc. Working in the "real" world automatically adds a timescale to an industrial project that just isn't there in the world of software development. Samples have to be physically transported from suppliers, manufacturing and delivery times have to be scheduled in. All of this time adds up. Because of this, there is only so much of the Agile/DevOps approach that can translate into the rest of industry, and so the speeded up "sprint" mechanism that Agile employs struggles to work in the rest of the industrial world. It's going to be much easier to maintain a sense of momentum on project delivery when the steps can be done on a daily or weekly basis, as with coding, but in a manufacturing industry, steps can take months to achieve due to the time lag in deliveries, assembly, etc., so it's naturally much tougher to maintain that sense of urgency. The second fundamental difference, is that in industry, the technical expertise required to do the R&D part of new product development tends to require highly specialist technical skills specific to that technology, e.g. a specialist in the chemistry of adhesives is unlikely to be able to design an aircraft engine, whereas in software, the technical skills of coding tend to be generic and can be applied, within the limits of programming languages, to almost any software development challenge. This therefore requires a different approach to team membership and resource allocation.

So – Agile versus waterfall – does it really matter? Both can succeed, both can fail. Whatever route you choose, success is less about the process itself, it's more about the people that are involved in it and how they own the process. So my take on Agile versus waterfall is that it does not really matter what label you want to use for your project management, as long as you approach it with structure, with discipline, with a dose of realism, as a team and above all, with the customer in mind.

4

THE THREE TIERS OF SUCCESSFUL INNOVATION

This whole book is built around the premise that becoming expert at the process of innovation is not, on its own, any guarantee to a business successfully growing through new products. To improve your chances of success, you also need to understand how your business's organisation and culture interact with the process and how they can serve to support or hinder innovation. So I think now is an appropriate time to introduce my "three tiers to successful innovation": organisation, process and culture. It's only when a business is in control of all three can it truly unlock its potential to grow through new products. We have explored in great detail in my previous book what we mean by the process of innovation – with a quick recap in Chapter 1 of this book – but what do we mean by organisation and culture? In this chapter, I want to define and expand on these concepts so that we are all clear as we move forward.

1) Organisation – we touched earlier on in this book about how successful innovation in a business requires a more collaborative structure

and a capability to manage the functional interfaces effectively, and we will explore in the next chapter how this contrasts with the more traditional hierarchical structure that most companies are still built around. These are all high-level aspects of what I mean when I am discussing the "organisation" of a business within this book. But once you look below the surface of these overall structural models of business, organisation means much more, especially to the individuals within the business.

a. Reporting lines – who is your boss? Who are your peers? Who is reporting in to you? Who are the key stakeholders and gatekeepers you need to influence? It doesn't matter whether you are the CEO, with a 40-year track record in industry, or whether it's your first day in your first job straight from college: knowing exactly where you fit in your company, and also in the wider market your business serves, is in fact vitally important if you want to be effective in doing your job, and that applies to "transforming technology into profit", as much as any role in the company.
b. Job roles – every role in any sizable, established business needs to have a job description of some kind, to establish clear boundaries so that you don't tread on others' toes. Otherwise it can lead to confusion, duplication of effort, things falling between the cracks and generally just annoying people – creating bad feelings and damaged relationships. In my own experience, the more senior the role, generally the more flexible and blurred are the boundaries of the job description, as more experienced people tend to appreciate that doing their job requires a degree of flexibility and stepping in to support other members of the team when needed, in order to get the job of doing business done. More junior staff, and early career people, tend to benefit from a more descriptive set of boundaries and objectives, because normally they have yet to develop the work ethic and personal discipline that usually only maturity and many years of working bring. There are exceptions of course, and it does depend on an individual's drive and capability as to how they are best constrained versus focused by a job description. Job descriptions and clarity of roles of course don't apply so much to small start-ups, as it has to be "all hands to the pumps" in

that environment. The bigger, the more complex and the more established the business, the more these rules will apply.

c. Ownership – another key aspect that I throw in to the "organisation" tier of successful innovation is somewhat related to and builds off job descriptions, and that is ownership. Job descriptions tend to contain ongoing guidelines of responsibilities and also touch on how the role should interact with other roles in a business, but these are not always directly relevant to every project or initiative that comes along, particularly when it relates to the various aspects of running new product or new business development projects and especially when it comes to business transformation initiatives to enhance the cultural aspects of innovation. Innovation by its very nature will produce things that can't always be anticipated and so cannot easily get written down on a job description. Clarifying exactly who is leading such initiatives and the autonomy they possess is essential not only for the person leading, but also for everyone else involved. Without clarity and communication of who is leading a project or initiative, there can be ambiguity of who is doing what, and potentially strong individuals can step in and take over (because that's their natural behaviour), even though it may not actually be their role and they may not be the best person for the particular job. Some things are obvious: the CTO/technical director will have ownership of the new product development portfolio, but who is responsible for commercialising those new products? Is it the CTO, is it the VP of sales, is it a combination or should it be delegated to someone else? These things need clarification, otherwise they will fall between the cracks, leading to under-delivery of projects and a finger-pointing culture. Ownership can be appointed by a senior figure or agreed by mutual consent – either works – as long as it is clear what is being owned and what they have to deliver.

d. Accountability – accountability is the next step from ownership and is about being responsible for delivering the results rather than leading/owning the project or initiative. Accountability and responsibility are often words used interchangeably, and whilst they share some aspects of meaning, they are subtly different. Accountability tends to be an individual thing, referring to the delivery aspect of owning or leading a project, whereas responsibility can be shared, with different team members being responsible for delivering sub-aspects of the whole initiative. Accountability is important because it builds trust in a team. Individuals who accept and are seen to take accountability for their results and their consequences, and who aren't quick to blame others when things don't go as planned, build integrity with their co-workers and enhance the collaborative spirit of a workplace.

e. Incentives – whether its ownership, accountability or responsibility you are referring to, they all get swept up into one thing when it comes to individual performance and their motivation to deliver on a task, and that is how they are remunerated and incentivised. All the previous aspects of organisation simply set the framework within which an individual has to perform. Who you report to, the relationship you have with them, the project ownerships that you are assigned or that you take on: all of these set the scene for you to do a job. How motivated you feel to do that job is linked to the emotional environment within which you are working, which can help you through the daily ups and downs of any job, but ultimately, medium- and long- term drive comes from the weekly or monthly pay packet that drops into your bank account, and to the bonuses that are directly linked to the results you deliver, be they business or project KPIs and targets.

f. Business strategy – I have written much in my previous book, *Transforming Technology into Profit*, on the importance of having a clear and communicated business strategy for your company, with a technology strategy to underpin in, and a practical implementation plan to make it all happen. Without a business strategy, it is really difficult for anyone working in the company to decide whether their daily actions are contributing to the success of the business or not, and when it comes to innovation, it makes it almost impossible to decide on which are the right ideas to take forward, and which are the right projects to back. So the business strategy forms the backdrop against which all the other aspects of organisation, process and culture must be held up for scrutiny.

2) Process – refer back to Chapter 1 for a summary of the key aspects of the process of innovation: idea generation, idea selection, project implementation and commercialisation and portfolio management.
3) Culture – I mention business culture frequently in this book, but what does this really mean? The culture of a business is the most intangible of all the three tiers of successful innovation to define. For a person like myself, who has made a career out of technology and business management, business can easily seem like a mechanical process, one that can be taught like a science, with a bit of "black art" thrown in, just like how to strip down and overhaul a car, and if you come from an engineering background, as many do in the world of industry, that's how you tend to view the world. And as this book is all about looking beyond the fence of technology, to see how it interacts and overlaps with other business functions, that's a relevant point of view to much of my readership. So to this all too common type of business person, culture is where all the "touchy-feely" stuff sits, where all the relationship and behavioural matters reside, and it can seem like a "black art". All this stuff can seem at first quite alien if you've been schooled in accounting, engineering, logistics, or some other discipline. But one thing I have learnt in the world of manufacturing when people claim something is a "black art", is that this is just a bland, fluffy phrase to hide the reality that the thing is just too complex for them to truly understand, and too difficult for them to be able to make real meaning of and to set rules to control it. You hear this phrase in industries based on formulation technologies, where highly complex, multi-ingredient mixtures are reduced to talk of sprinkling "foo foo dust" in, and in manufacturing processes where there are just so many variables at play that no one has bothered to do the hard slog of investigating how they all interact. And so it is the same with culture, with behaviours and with relationships. After all, humans are the most complex machines of all. But it doesn't have to be like that. Behavioural science and leadership psychology have come a long way in documenting and categorising behavioural types and personality preferences, and there is much that can be learnt to aid innovation by looking under the lid of how people interact with each other in highly collaborative business situations.
   a. Team dynamics – success in creating and commercialising new products will only come from a team effort. It certainly requires

strong leadership to keep the team on track and deliver to targets and timescales, but the range of skills you will need to get the job done is extensive. So how that team interacts, how well they communicate with each other, how effectively they work with each other, both when they are in a room together, or working remotely from each other, has a massive influence on how well – and even if – you deliver what you set out to. This is team dynamics, but how do you understand what is going on with all your team members? How do you get to analyse their behaviours, their personality traits and how complementary or how divisive they are together? Fortunately, behavioural science can help tremendously these days with a multitude of analysis tools (e.g. FIRO or Belbin) that help you dig deep into the psyche of you and your team members and point you in the direction of where areas of conflict are most likely to arise. The big challenge though is what you do with all this information once you have it. It's all very well to have well-constructed and researched models and tests to probe behaviours, but the average business or project leader is rarely equipped to know what to do with the output. This is the harder part, as for those without natural people skills, it requires years of building empathy, maturity and experience, coupled with targeted training on how to put the results and guidance into practice with real people in a real work environment.

b. Collaboration – collaboration is what happens when two or more people try to work together to achieve a common goal. Typically this will happen within the team environment, so collaboration is naturally happening, and has to happen for the team to achieve its common purpose. A team can only hope to deliver if they work together effectively. But for me, collaboration is more than that, it is also about sparking off each other creatively, creating something more than the sum of the parts. It is not just following normal procedures together, which any group of sufficiently trained people can do, it is not just about crunching numbers to get the expected output. And some people just naturally work well together in this way, feeding off each other's energies and creativity to build up ideas and procedures into something better, something more efficient than existed before. And everyone has met people like that, people that you either work with now or have worked with in the past, people you just naturally get on well with, with whom you have a more energetic, free-flowing exchange of ideas, and a positive "collaborative" discussion that leads somewhere new. But it's not just something that happens between two individuals in a team, every business has collaboration going on every day between every set of individuals and teams that work together, and outside in their interactions with customers and suppliers, but what makes the difference is the "quality" of collaboration: that is what all businesses are striving for these days. Unfortunately, collaboration is another much overused business buzzword these days, with different meanings to different people, and so the first step to improve collaboration in your business is simply deciding on a relevant definition. Collaboration can be measured in a variety of ways, but again, the measurements need to be relevant to your business, to your definition and targeted to guide the behaviour you are aiming for. One key thing needed to improve the quality of collaboration within any business is simply to get people to interact more frequently, and in the right way, so they can grow their network and build relationships, which presents an increasing challenge in a business world where remote working and geographically spread teams become more common. Creativity is one thing, and there are techniques developed to help enhance an individual's creativity, but collaboration takes that and builds on it to enhance a group's ability to create something more. And so many of the techniques used to manage and improve team dynamics and the information derived from understanding behavioural preferences contributes to improving collaboration within a business. Collaboration by its nature requires overlap, and so it's no surprise that collaboration sits at the interface of many of the concepts, themes and models we have explored in this book. To get better at collaboration, you need to consider team dynamics, thinking styles and behavioural preferences, you need to consider organisational structure and management of the functional interfaces and plenty of other aspects we have discussed in this book.

c. Thinking styles/behavioural preferences – when you have run all the way through from the front to the end of the process of innovation a few times, one thing that strikes you when trying to create and successfully commercialise new products is the diversity and range of skills that are required to move from one end to the other. Just consider the type of person you need at the front end. This stage is all about generating ideas (and lots of them), in a relatively unfettered way, blinkers off, no holds barred. You need creative, freethinking people, comfortable with exploring abstract concepts without setting too many rules or boundaries and without being overly judgemental on the ideas. This style of thinking is known as "divergent thinking", and you need people like this to fill your innovation funnel. In contrast, once the funnel is full and you have gone through your idea selection process and launched a few new product development projects, the last people you want are divergent thinkers. By then, you are in implementation stage and to progress down the funnel you need hard action and project execution. So what you need is doers, people who are much more comfortable working within tight boundaries, setting and working to achieve clear targets, to defined timescales. This style of thinking is called "convergent thinking". This is where you need your engineers, keen to dive into a task, set a plan and get started making it happen. And once the engineers have created and productionised the new product, and the project has progressed towards commercialisation, you then need the next type of person, the relationship builder, to target customers and sell the concept to the market place. These three types of behavioural and thinking preferences are an oversimplification of the range and diversity of skills and styles you need, but you get the picture. Successful innovation is a long hard road and requires team effort. And because it's a long road, you need to be aware that the team roles may need to change as the project progresses. So knowing the skills and preferences of the individuals at your disposal in the business is important when trying to build the right team for the task at hand, and also understanding when the right skills are absent and that you might need to hire or go outside for expert consultancy.

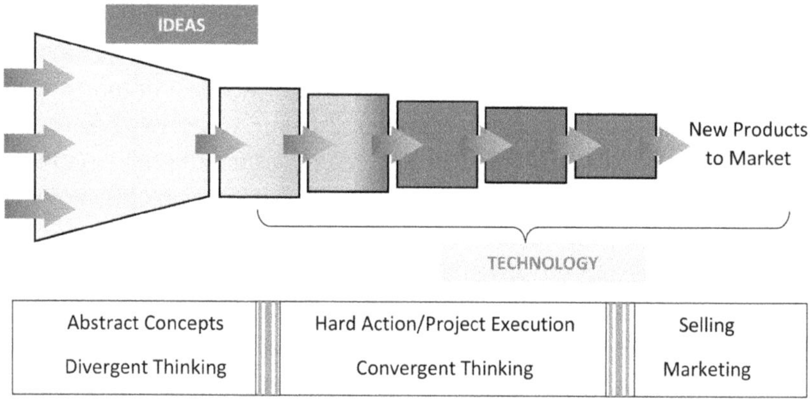

The "three tiers to successful innovation" can be summed up in one simple graphic:

5

ORGANISATIONAL SCHIZOPHRENIA – YOUR TWO COMPETING ORGANISATIONS

> The knowledge processes required for 'learning by doing' ('exploitation' of existing capabilities) are very different from those required for searching and developing new opportunities for value creation ('exploration').
>
> James Hayton, Pro Dean, University of Warwick Business School

After many years of experiencing successes and failures with trying to grow business revenue and profit by developing and introducing new products, one fundamental reality I came to understand was that in every mature business I have ever worked in or with, there are actually two organisations competing for air space. Sometimes fighting against each other, sometimes ignoring each other, sometimes trying to work together, but more often than not these two organisations are frequently out of sync by some degree, which is where I came to realise the fundamental problem lies in trying to grow your business, and that problem is inside your own business, not out there in the marketplace. This is something I have observed over my 30 years in business, working in lots of different companies, so it cannot just be a one-off problem, it is a situation that appears to pervade many, many businesses, and if I assume that the businesses I have worked with are not that different from many others, so by extrapolation, I assume this is a universal problem, backed up by numerous conversations on this subject with colleagues at conferences and business events.

What I have seen firsthand is that having these two competing organisations within your business out of synchronisation is what leads to all of those "internal factors" that have been identified early on in this book as being the root cause of why most businesses struggle to grow. Having two organisations locked within your business is almost like the company having two personalities, each fighting for dominance and each occasionally taking the lead depending on how well developed the business is, but ultimately locked in a constant battle for supremacy. Since I got to the point in my career that I began to realise that this situation exists, and then to develop my thoughts to the point of formulating this into an observation that I could explain in simple terms, I have had the chance to discuss this with the senior academic faculty of the innovation department at Warwick University Business School. They call this the "ambidexterity problem", but I prefer to call this situational challenge "organisational schizophrenia", because when you're on one side of the divide trying to make yourself heard within a business, it really does feel like a fight. (Yes, I know schizophrenia is not technically multiple personality disorder, but most people, erroneously, associate it with the condition, so they relate to the phrase – plus it sounds cooler). So what are these two competing organisations within your business? I call them the "day-to-day" organisation and the "innovation" organisation.

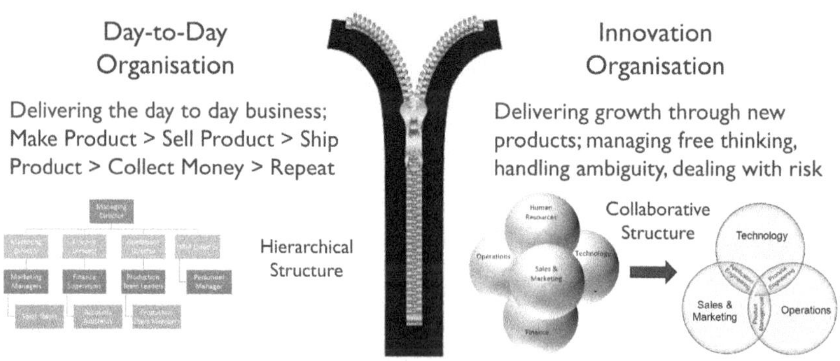

The day-to-day part of your business is that which is focused on the standard product lines that are the bedrock of any mature business. It is focused on the process of "make product > sell product > ship product > collect money > repeat". To drive this type of organisation forward, it works continuously on making that process as efficient and cost-effective as possible, driving costs down, driving productivity up and optimising price. This is the traditional model of any mature business, built around a classic hierarchical organisational structure.

The innovation organisation is that part of your business that is focused on delivering growth through new products. This type of organisation is fundamentally different from the day-to-day organisation, because it needs to be able to handle freethinking (for idea generation), and handle much higher levels of ambiguity and risk (as many ideas and projects will not make it to commercialisation) than the day-to-day organisation. And so an innovation organisation works best with a more collaborative structure, a type of structure that many businesses struggle to conceptualise. We explored this in Chapter 2 of this book and in my previous book *Transforming Technology into Profit*.

And this is the fundamental practical challenge for any business. You have two aspects to your business – two personalities if you will – but you need both types of organisation to be successful. You need to be bringing in money from your day-to-day business, and delivering future growth through your innovation organisation. This is the key to having a successful thriving business today and delivering profitable sustainable growth long into the future. But because the two halves of your organisation are fundamentally different in structure and in the types of behaviours and skills that are needed, they seem almost incompatible and almost every business therefore struggles to manage the dichotomy. Being able to manage this effectively is the key to unlocking the true potential of your business to growth through new products. And the first step to doing this is to recognise that you have this situation deep-rooted within your business.

The success of your business is going to be dependent on how well the day-to-day and innovation organisations within your business are synchronised. This is what generates directly all those "internal factors" we have been alluding to throughout this book. Every mature business has some degree of synchronisation, whether it is very poor or very good, and like many things it is not black or white, it is a continuum. There is no ideal, 100% perfectly aligned business. Sure, we should strive to attain that, but you are never going to get there for many practical reasons, but that's okay. No business has to be perfect, you just need to recognise the situation, make changes, and improve your synchronisation to deliver tangible improvements to your business' performance. And equally, there is no business that is zero percent synchronised, otherwise they would not exist in business. All businesses are somewhere along the continuum. So let's explore what good and bad looks like, what it feels like to work in such extremes of organisation and how such businesses are likely to look from the outside and how they will perform.

Poor Organisational Synchronisation

If you work in a business with poorly synchronised day-to-day and innovation organisations, you are likely to experience a whole raft of internal inefficiencies. You will likely work in an environment that is heavily internally focused, and you will find yourself going to too many meetings. Your business will suffer from poor collaboration and there will be frequent duplication of effort as isolated teams struggle with common, but unshared tasks, and a general lack of common goals across the business. Your business will have some good people with good ideas, but their ideas will just seem to disappear into a corporate black hole, never seeing the light of day, discouraging idea generation and general participation. The working culture may seem somewhat toxic to some individuals, who at best will feel ignored. This is just a very short list of some of the "internal factors" that are holding back growth in your business if you have poor alignment of the two halves of your organisation.

In terms of performance, from the outside you will see a business that is too slow in bringing new products to market, if they do at all, and if they do manage to bring new products to market, product performance and revenue generations will frequently fall short of expectations. You might also see a business that manages some form of new product development and R&D programme, but this will tend to deliver "technical successes, commercial failures" (see Chapter 3 for examples of my own technical successes, commercial failures). And generally you will see a business that is underdelivering on its new business development plans.

Good Organisational Synchronisation

By contrast, if you are lucky enough to work in a business which has good synchronisation between its day-to-day and innovation organisations, you are likely to work in an environment that has clearly documented and well managed innovation processes, shared across the whole organisation. Your employees will enjoy high levels of effective collaboration. There will be clear accountability and ownership of projects and initiatives, and there will be shared goals which contribute directly and tangibly to a clear business strategy.

From the outside, you will see a business that has visible innovation metrics with targets, and has a clear technology strategy that underpins the overall business strategy, along with a practical implementation plan to make it happen. You will see performance against the plan reported regularly throughout the organisation and reviewed as a regular agenda item at each board meeting. And ultimately, you will see a business that has increasing new product sales and that is adding new profitable revenue streams to its portfolio.

Most mature businesses will be somewhere along the continuum between these two extremes. Every business has some good aspects to their processes, the way they are organised and their culture, and likewise, every business has areas they can improve. Having a starting and an end point helps enormously, and allows you to create an improvement plan. This is the power of the day-to-day/innovation organisations concept, because this gives you a framework around which to build a plan. Once you develop an understanding of how well the two organisations are synchronised within your organisation, this gives you the starting point, from which you can work to progress towards full synchronisation.

I keep stressing so far in this chapter that this concept is most relevant to "mature" businesses. Every business will naturally go through a maturity cycle, and I have dealt with businesses which are only innovation organisations or are only day-to-day organisations. Start-ups are by their very nature innovation organisations, they are developing a product (be it a physical thing or a service) or a suite of products. They normally start off with a small team, which works in a highly collaborative way, with highly flexible, entrepreneurial individuals, and form a small collaborative organisation as described earlier, that underpins the innovation part of any business. Assuming the start-up gets off the ground and builds sales, reputation and market presence, the initial product offering becomes mature and eventually becomes standard products for the business. Then the start-up has to develop systems, processes and a structure to efficiently deliver these products to their customers in a cost-effective way, at which point the day-to-day part of the organisation is born. What can happen when such a business morphs from an innovation organisation to a day-to-day organisation is that it can stay there locked into day-to-day mode, and I have certainly worked with companies that only seem to be day-to-day organisations. This can happen for a variety of reasons, such as the company is bought by a third party and the original entrepreneurial founders leave the business, taking the drive for innovation with them. Or the original founder retires and the business appoints a seasoned business manager to run the business, rather than another entrepreneurial type. Such businesses can sustain a profitable income for the lifetime of their natural product lifecycle, after which they will become extinct. Every product is a time-limited opportunity to make money. It might be three to five years for a consumer electronic product, or it might be a couple of centuries for foundry crucibles.

In some cases, some start-ups never ever get out of innovation mode, and limp along, existing on one government grant after another.

During the middle of my career, I witnessed firsthand the struggle between the entrepreneurial innovation style of organisation and the day-to-day organisation when the large global corporate I was working for acquired a small independent manufacturing business in Germany. The small German business had been built up into a very profitable twenty million euro turnover company, supplying products to foundries all over the world. The owner, though not the original founder, had been the heir apparent of the previous owning family, who had sold the business to him twenty years previously. He was a classic entrepreneur, with a very strong personality, and with an attitude that his way was always the right way. My boss at the time, who lead the acquisition, the president of our global division, was a very solid business manager, a very safe pair of hands, and a classic day-to-day organisational hierarchical leader. Both very strong businessmen, but absolutely poles apart in their attitudes, their styles and the way they thought a business should be run. I was the technology director of the global division at this time, and it was my role to integrate the new German business' materials, products and processes into our global division. A tough job when the German company boss always thought their technology was better than ours on every front, but still, perseverance, planning and relationship building with the German management team got us there.

The whole integration process took at least two years, and at times was very uncomfortable on both sides, especially for the German boss and his team. It was during this period that I really learnt the huge challenges of getting two very different styles of business to work in synchronisation. The German business was much more of an innovation style of organisation (with a small dose of day-to-day organisation), whereas our global corporate was much more of a day-to-day organisation (with a small dose of innovation organisation). And for those individuals that would be affected by the integration process, if all you have experienced is working your whole career in that business, you think that is normal, you think your style of organisation and culture is normal, and it is hard to empathise with those working within a different business, with its different structure and different culture. For the two businesses, the integration slowly happened, the two businesses slowly synchronised. Business processes were aligned, raw material sources were combined, technologies were transferred between sites, but still there remained cultural differences, some of which would and maybe could never be fully assimilated. We were dealing with multiple geographical sites, different nationalities and different cultural perceptions for individuals, after all.

Yes, we were ultimately successful with the integration, with a lot of time, planning and sensitivity to how the change was going to affect everyone; it is possible to integrate and synchronize two different styles of business, two types of organisation, but probably the single most important lesson I learnt from this episode in my career is just how much influence the person at the top has on the nature of a business. The boss sets the tone, sets the structure, and their personal style and attitude largely sets the character of the culture of the entire business. The strong personalities and deep-rooted business styles and attitudes of both my boss (the divisional president) and the boss of the German business were the biggest barrier to integration of all. These two individuals were always very civil and professional to each other, but because of their very different styles, they never really saw eye to eye on anything, and it was obvious in every meeting we ever sat through, every conversation we were ever party to and every dinner we attended together. The entrepreneurial German boss really struggled with handing over power, handing over the running of his business to a higher authority. Though I am not sure what he expected, he was after all selling his business, pocketing his money – did he just expect the new owners to just give him the money and leave him alone? I did think there was a touch of naivety on his part about this. My boss, the divisional president, certainly displayed a huge amount of patience with the whole situation, I am sure he saw the pain that the German boss was going through and understood that integration would ultimately require perseverance, relationship building and some tough decisions. One decision that was a sticking point for a long time was that the German boss expected his son, the sales manager at the time, to take over his role running the company when he retired. My boss was not having any of this of course, this type of nepotism just can't be tolerated within a corporate environment, something which the German boss, with his local, family style ownership experience, could never really accept. This clash between the two bosses was always the biggest barrier and the final hurdle to overcome, and it never truly got addressed, right up until the point that the German boss retired, about four years after the acquisition. At that point the divisional president was free to appoint his own man into the German site and extend his own style of day-to-day organisation more fully, and the integration was finally complete.

But looking beyond the boss problem, why is it so difficult to get the two halves of any organisation in synchronisation? There are numerous reasons, but the most important ones are all people related. One of the most fundamental of challenges is that those people working in the day-to-day side of the business are very happy doing their jobs every day, getting paid at the end of the week or month, and just getting on with life, thank you very much. The very nature of the innovation organisation side of the business means that whatever comes out of there is going to have a profound effect on what those individuals in the day-to-day side of the business do. If the innovation organisation is successful at what they do, then it has the potential to massively change what the day-to-day people do, and most of these people do not like the thought of this. Why? Because the people that thrive within day-to-day or innovation organisations are very different types of people. Those in the day-to-day side are usually the types of people that are great at doing routine, regular tasks, to set procedures. That is not to say that they don't also work to continuously strive to improve those processes, it doesn't mean they are complacent, but just that they are good at building efficient, effective routines. This is what is needed to keep costs down in an organisation, supporting good business management and contributing to profitability. In contrast, the types of people that thrive within an innovation environment are those that actively crave change, that need a constant stream of new challenges and problems to stimulate their minds. Unfortunately, for any business, these two types of people do not naturally work effectively together, and it requires much cultural and behavioural work before the thinkers and the doers empathise sufficiently with each other to appreciate the skills and contribution that the other brings.

As I have stated before in this book, most company CEOs make the mistake that they think the innovation part of their business is purely the realm of the CTO, and that they should leave them alone to run with it. One of the reasons that this is a mistake is that this can too easily build up a day-to-day versus innovation organisational divide, effectively creating two silos and splitting the company, not quite down the middle, because the split is rarely even. For some individuals, their roles within the organisation will quite clearly place them on one side or other of this divide, and an "us and them" mentality can arise. But since we have already touched on the fact several times in this, and in my previous book, that collaboration and innovation happen at the functional interfaces between departments, this also crosses over the day-to-day/innovation organisational divide. So for many individuals, the lines between the two organisations can seem blurred, especially when it comes to accountability, ownership and reporting lines, and some individuals will find themselves with a foot in both camps, though their personal allegiance is almost inevitably with one or the other depending on their career background and mindset.

At the other end of the scale, there are those CEOs who embrace the whole concept of innovation to such an extent that they want to transform the whole of their business into an innovation organisation, usually accompanied with a headline vision to become a more "agile" organisation, or similar statement, and a drive to push through Agile or lean start-up methodologies throughout the business, irrespective of whether they are on the day-to-day or the innovation side of the organisation. I also see this as a mistake because as the two parts of the business are fundamentally different, they therefore require different approaches to optimise them, and are best served by employing bespoke business processes and methodologies tailored specifically to them, not a one-size-fits-all approach. I believe it stems from the fundamental misinterpretation of "Agile" the brand versus "agile" the adjective (see explanation in Chapter 3).

I have been in the unique position in my career of having to lead both types of organisation, so I have seen the divide from both sides of the fence and from both points of view. I think this is what has given me such a unique perspective and a unique vantage point from which to identify and observe the issue with organisational schizophrenia that every company has to deal with. And also to appreciate that you need both styles of organisation within a company for a mature business to both thrive today and grow tomorrow.

Organisational Structure in an Ever-Changing World

Chris Parr, VP Science & Technology at Imerys Aluminates, part of the French-based global multinational Imerys Group, that we met in Chapter

3, has experienced a variety of organisational changes in his career. During our earlier discussions on "technical successes, commercial failures", we also got onto the topic of how structure influences the ability of a business to innovate effectively, and Chris explained some of the real-world challenges he has experienced in trying to lead innovation in an ever changing corporate world.

At one stage of his career, Chris worked in a large multinational that was expanding considerably through acquisition, bringing with it the constant challenge of integration of each new business that comes along into the organisational structure and culture. In terms of one practical aspect of how this affects innovation, each acquisition of an existing business brings with it yet another R&D centre, and yet another decision on how to absorb the assets into the current technology function, which also includes dealing with all the new people. In a big corporate giant, with multiple sites in a variety of countries, it is not always easy to move people around the world. An organisational structure that might look good on paper is not always so practical to deliver. And throughout this period of perpetual integration of new businesses, the company also underwent significant changes in leadership, bringing with it new approaches and new strategic directions, and a merry-go-round of organisational changes.

Chris has observed that many giant corporations that have been around for a long time tend to dominate their market segments, finding themselves with little room to grow, and so periodically explore diversification as a means to deliver growth. One typical approach to this is for the business to set up a centralised innovation centre to focus on identifying and developing medium/long term strategic new markets. This usually requires significant organisational reconfiguration and a major shift in focus for the R&D team to gear up to access new markets. But long term strategic initiatives need long-term support to have any hope of delivering their objectives, and there is no way that such an organisational experiment in strategy and business development can possibly deliver in less than two years. The redirection in strategy that can come from top-level leadership changes mid-programme, too often results in a dramatic reversal in approach and a decision to close and dismantle such innovation centres before they have had any chance to deliver. Closing an innovation centre has an immediate write-off cost of abandonment, but it can also have a much wider, longer lasting effect to the organisation beyond the investment write-off, because with such organisational experimenting also comes the high cost of people experiments, changing roles and locations, which means major upheavals to an individual's lives and their families.

Chris' experience highlights the real-world challenges of maintaining control and direction when the world around you is changing rapidly, and that relates to both structure and culture, and it is a situation mirrored in many companies, both large and small, all over the world. It is all very well having a strategy and an implementation plan, but there are always multiple external and internal pressures constantly acting on a business' ability to stick to that plan.

Whatever the plan, having some period of consistency is usually a necessity if a business wants to deliver on the goals it has set itself but the pace of change, both within a corporate environment and within the outside world of the markets they play in, brings constant pressure, which makes maintaining consistency a huge challenge for any management team. And whatever the leadership decides, down in the actual business, employees of a business invariably welcome some period of consistency simply to absorb and act on the latest initiative from on high. New masters usually mean new initiatives, and it is easy for long-term employees to get "initiative fatigue" as year on year they see yet another edict from the top pushed down into the business, only to be junked and replaced one or two years later.

Change may be the norm these days, but how can you deliver stability and consistency of approach when the person at the top is changing, when the strategy is changing, when the game plan is changing. And change from integrating acquisitions also inevitably leads to people turnover, either from those pushed out due to redundancy or those dissatisfied with the changes and instability, increasing risk from loss of specialist skills and industry knowledge, particularly when it comes to the specialist technical skills necessary to develop new technologies and products.

Organisational Synchronisation – Case Study

One of the ways in which we can perhaps better appreciate the challenge of managing through the day-to-day versus the innovation organisation paradox, is to dig deeper into real-life examples. By considering how different companies attempted to deal with this, what challenges they faced and what the consequences were, we can hopefully learn a few useful lessons. But remember, there is no one-size-fits-all solution, and every company is different, so case studies should not be used as "cut and paste" exercises for your own business.

One of my contacts, Ian Sterritt, related to me an interesting and very relevant story about one of his past experiences early on in his career. Ian has over 30 years' experience leading innovation activities in a variety of automotive and industrial companies, and is a big supporter of tech start-ups, so knows what he is talking about when it comes to business innovation.

Right at the start of the 2000's, Ian got involved with a major diversification project for London Taxis International, the world recognised manufacturer of black cabs, based in Coventry (UK), and part of Manganese Bronze Holdings plc. Black cab taxis are highly unique vehicles in terms of design and manufacture because they need to comply with specific taxi legislation laid down by Transport for London, the local government body responsible for the transport system in Greater London. This legislation requires certain features to be present in the vehicle which standard passenger vehicles would not normally have, such as the tightness of the turning circle, plus numerous safety features. This unique market situation meant that London Taxi International was a truly niche manufacturer, producing around 1,500 vehicles per year at the time.

Due to the unique market niche that London Taxi International played in, and the fact that they had to work within the Transport for London regulations, the Chairman of the Board recognised that this represented a massive strategic risk to the business. If Transport for London decided to change their regulations, that could have a huge impact on their business costs, and if they decided to open the market to other players, that could potentially close down their business almost overnight, a business that was valued around £32m at the time.

The Chairman, and main private shareholder of the company, was Jamie Borwick, a career British businessman who is also a hereditary peer (Fifth Baron Borwick), and was elected to the House of Lords in 2013. During the late 1990s, he convinced the board at the time of the huge strategic risk that the company faced and started to search for ways to inoculate the business, by diversifying and reinventing for the future. In 1999, the task was given to the company's Business Development Director to go and seek opportunities for diversification, with the usual remit of "but don't spend too much money on it".

This is where my friend Ian Sterritt entered the story. During the Business Development Director's travels, he bumped into Ian at an event at Warwick University. They got to talking. Ian had recently been doing some work with Philips Electronics, working on commercialising the first generation satellite navigation consumer products in the UK market. Their conversation sparked some potential ideas for a new direction for London Taxi International, and Ian was appointed as a consultant to help the business develop new technology, new products and a new business model. They worked for eighteen months on technical and commercial feasibility studies, and building a business proposition.

During this period, London Taxi International was very heavily a day-to-day organisation, with a well-hidden innovation organisation only serving to drip feed slow evolution of their existing products onto the market. What Ian and the team were doing was an attempt at a radical rethink of the business' product offering and business model, so right from the start it was understood by the board that this had to be something organisationally separate, to avoid the day-to-day of the business influencing what they were trying to achieve. They accomplished this by setting up a dedicated, embryonic team in a stand-alone warehouse on the Coventry factory site, converted into appropriate office space and support facilities, to deliberately isolate it from the rest of the company. The team started with some employees moved over from the main business to get them off the ground, but these were quickly supported by the new specialists that were actually needed to progress the technological developments required to create the new products that would be the foundation of the new business direction. Once the team and facility had got off the ground, operational involvement from the main business was kept to a bare minimum. This situation essentially gave the new innovation team free range to do whatever they deemed strategically necessary.

One reason that the team was stand-alone from the rest of the business, and required dedicated new employees, was that the technology they were working on was completely different from the automotive engineering skills that were the mainstream of London Taxi International at the time, and so appropriate technical skills had to be sought from outside. The new technology was to use mobile phone networks to triangulate where the passenger was located when they made a phone call for a taxi, and then to locate the nearest free taxi to service that passenger. This seems commonplace now with the likes of Uber, but it was ground-breaking stuff nearly twenty years ago. For a taxi cab company, such technology could provide a revolutionary new service, and this is what the team worked so hard to develop.

The team spent the first few months developing the business proposition, but because it was such a radical idea and employed what might as well have been alien technology to the rest of the board, at first, few of the senior team in the organisation really understood what they were trying to do, and more importantly, why they should continue to spend money on it. There was plenty of politics at play in the senior team, and ultimately the scheme did move forward, principally because it was the pet project of the Chairman. Eventually, after much discussion, initial seed funding was provided to develop the business case, structure the business plan, and create a detailed technology roadmap and route to market plan.

As the project progressed, and the board were kept updated through regular monthly updates, slowly they all came to understand the strategic risk and to back the project. What also no doubt helped a lot was the strong personal relationship the project director had with the owner, which kept him closely informed, and the project constantly on the board's agenda. But whilst the project was slowly winning the hearts and minds of the board members, the main business' operational team were still largely kept out of the loop and consequently were not very supportive of the efforts that were going on to create an innovative new future for the business. There were occasions when the team were forced to use the Chairman's personal direct sponsorship of the programme as a "joker card" to get what they needed from the main business.

One fundamental question that arises from this case study – that is applicable to any new product development programme and to any radical new business model – is: is it right to completely isolate the new business and product development team from the rest of the main business? It's a real-life practical dilemma that every business faces with any major new project and initiative, not just new product innovations.

Keeping the new project team unencumbered by the day-to-day business must certainly help to maintain focus on their key task and give the project every chance of progressing quickly. If innovation team members also have jobs in the day-to-day part of the business, there is an inevitable dilemma that such people will face every day about what they should be working on, what they should prioritise. But if the team is kept cut off from the rest of the main business, then those individuals working in the day-to-day business inevitably develop an unhealthy attitude about "what's going on over there?", "why are they spending all this money?", "what are they trying to achieve?", "how is it going to affect our business?", and most importantly, "how is it going to affect me?"

Keeping people in the dark always means that they will speculate and make up information in the absence of it, and usually not in a positive way. So whilst keeping the innovation team isolated may speed up progress on the project, the lack of ongoing communication with the rest of the business inevitably builds an attitudinal barrier that amounts to tangible resistance when it comes to integration and deployment of the project outcome, slowing down implementation. So an isolationist approach to innovation can be a double-edged sword. The reality is that there is no single right answer to this situation. A judgement has to be made for each case, as the right approach will depend on many things, such as the available resources, the scale and complexity of the business, the availability and scale of finance needed, etc.

The fact that the London Taxi International new business development project team had been set up in a separate unit, with stand-alone resources, and now with funding available, meant that the project progressed quickly. But when it came to getting out to the market and interfacing with potential customers and end users, the team had to start interacting more closely with the rest of the mainstream business for access, and that's when the first operational barriers went up. The Head of Sales was a particular challenge, with an all too common attitude that I have personally encountered many times in many businesses. Conversations to ask about approaching customers to trial the new technology would typically open with phrases like "I've been in this business for 25 years, don't start telling me about my customers", or "Don't you dare stop me selling any more taxis with your tinpot new ideas". The head of sales is almost always a critical gatekeeper to win over in any new product development process: they can make or break your project. Getting them involved as early as possible in the project, preferably at the idea selection stage, is a good way to get them aligned, supportive and contributing, but in this case, this was not the way the business chose to pursue this new opportunity, a consequence of which was this confrontational stage, and a need to find some way to win over the individual.

The way that Ian eventually got the head of sales on board was by demonstrating the new team's professionalism and capability, and by dealing with the incumbent sales team as colleagues, not adversaries, offering something of real value to them, something that would help them in doing their own job and delivering their own goals. Ian went out to the market and analysed the demographics of the 18,000 taxi drivers in London. He created a market segmentation analysis that identified those types of drivers that would likely be resistant to the new technology and those willing to try new things based on the value of the technology, along with a targeted plan on how to approach them and convert them first into trials and then into customers. After six months of hard work, the analysis identified five different market segments, which on presenting to the head of sales, proved to be a turning point. Immediately the person could see the value that this new information brought to his own role. The business had never done anything like this before, and the analysis gave the head of sales a completely new insight into the taxi driver market and offered clear and managed commercialisation plans for both the existing business and the new technology. This activity proved highly effective in neutralising the main internal opposition to progressing the new ride hailing system through the company and out to the market.

There are always plenty of sensitivities to consider when pursuing radical new business models and when introducing radical new products that have the potential to change the very nature of a business, and consequently the roles of individuals within that business. And in changing the nature of roles, it changes the nature of individual's remuneration and future career prospects, which is always at the forefront of any person's mind when they see potential change heading their way. "What does it mean to me?"; "How will it affect me?" This is fair enough, there is not one person in a business that doesn't think this way, including the people leading the change. Successfully creating new products and business models is an exercise in effective project management, but successfully implementing them is an exercise in change management.

Memorably for the team, the board meeting at which formal approval for their new mobile phone based taxi hailing system was given the go-ahead and the first of several of funding tranches allocated, was on the day of the infamous 9/11 attacks (11 September 2001). The board was meeting in London, and after winning approval, the team stepped out onto the streets of central London, only to find them eerily deserted. Unbeknownst to them, the 9/11 attacks were potentially considered to be part of a wider attack on global financial centres, and so the City (London's financial district) had been evacuated. We all remember where we were on 9/11 (personally, I was swimming in a pool in Florida on vacation, when an American woman came running out of the apartments shouting, "We're at war", "We're at war").

The whole project, from the initial conversation that sparked the concept, to formal product launch, took around four years. A new company was created to manage the new business, called Zingo. Products hit the streets in October 2002, and following successful trials with passengers and drivers, a high profile, multi-channel publicity campaign was launched across London early in 2003. Demand from passengers quickly grew, as did demand from taxi drivers to have the system fitted into their cabs, and the system went on to win mobile phone industry new disruptive technology awards.

I was particularly keen to include this real-life business innovation project scenario as a case study in this book because it incorporates several of the themes I have written about in both my previous book, *Transforming Technology into Profit*, and in this new book, and also highlights the challenges that mature businesses face in trying to manage the day-to-day versus the innovation facets of their organisation. But the story is not over, there is one final twist, and one further valuable learning point to be made.

This case study reads like a classic great idea that struggled through multiple challenges but which, through the dedication, professionalism and talent of a few key individuals, eventually succeeded, and succeed it did, at first. Once it was past the early adopter phase, demand for the new service skyrocketed, leading to a huge demand to place the equipment into taxis. But demand was such that the business quickly ran into a cash flow problem and just could not finance the production of sufficient systems quickly enough to keep up. At the point of commercial launch, the parent company had sunk £15m into Zingo. Every possible asset it owned was mortgaged to the max to fund the new venture, putting a huge financial strain on London Taxi International. Demand far outstripped sales projections and their ability to finance the growth, so Zingo just ran out of money. In its final year, it reported a loss of £4m, a huge drain on the holding company Manganese Bronze, who eventually decided to cut their losses and sold Zingo to ComfortDelGro, a Singapore-owned transport company, for just £1. (As a strange aside, in a "it's a small world" twist of fate, ComfortDelGro is actually one of the few taxi hailing apps I have on my phone today, having used it regularly over the last eight years in my numerous business trips to Singapore). The whole concept of Zingo was ahead of its time, as one of the first mobile-based taxi hailing systems available. Nowadays, technology has moved on, and such things seem routine thanks to the latest smartphone technology and the numerous taxi apps available in almost every country you visit.

The financial failure of Zingo, coupled with dwindling taxi sales for London Taxi International, and an unsuccessful boardroom coup by the owner, Jamie Borwick, was all too much for the firm. Borwick resigned as Chairman early in 2003, and after two unsuccessful attempts to buy the rest of the parent company's shares and take it private, decided to sell all his holdings early in 2004 and walked away. To prop up the business, and gain better access to overseas markets, London Taxi International subsequently formed a joint venture with Geely, a large Chinese automotive manufacturer, who set up production of black cabs for export markets at a facility in Shanghai. Geely increasingly dominated the partnership and in 2013 bought the company outright. In 2017 it renamed the business the London EV Company and refocused the Coventry plant on developing electric commercial vehicles.

Key Learnings

1) The ability to continuously finance growth is critical to build on your initial successes.
2) A drive from the top is essential to force radical innovation.
3) The value of regular and strong channels of communication with the decision makers and key stakeholders.

6

HOW TO IDENTIFY THE BARRIERS HOLDING BACK INNOVATION

> We're always increasing the speed of innovation investments on growth, so our organization is perpetually adjusting to maximize impact. This strategy allows us to stay relevant to our customers so we can enable their success in innovation-driven markets.
>
> Alexa Dembek, Chief Technology and Sustainability Officer at DuPont

How good is your business at innovation? How good is your business at generating ideas and transforming them into profitable new products? You will surely have an opinion on this, as will everyone else in your business, but they will probably all be different. And so you likely don't have a definitive answer to this, especially if you do not measure KPIs related to this, or maybe you don't measure KPIs at all? How good is your business? I can already tell you the answer: not as good as it should be, and not as good as it could be. So what's the secret? How do businesses get better at innovation? There are three ways to work up to an answer:

1) Look back at your own career, to understand what you learnt along the way, assess your successes and failures and learn from them, as I have done in Chapters 2 and 3 of this book.
2) Get feedback from colleagues, and from your wider network, on your own experiences. Listen to the experiences of others and compare and contrast with your own, as I have done in several sections of this book.
3) By studying case studies of how other businesses have made a success or failure of innovation, and there are several such case studies distributed throughout this book. Let's take a look at one such example.

A Case Study in the Challenges of Diversification – Intel

Intel is a great recent example of a giant corporation which stopped innovating effectively and suffered very quickly as a consequence. Intel placed too few bets on too few product groups and poured billions into extra production capacity to support them. Sure, it has been very busy trying to innovate over recent time, dabbling at diversification, but history shows its efforts proved ineffective. Intel failed to see that it had stopped truly innovating. It took some notice of what was over the market horizon and where it should be headed next, but failed to act and/or was frequently too slow in responding, and yet again, is currently desperately scrambling around to find the next big thing to diversify its product portfolio.

I witnessed firsthand Intel's rise to glory whilst I was based in China. I lived in a city called Dalian, in the North East of China, in Liaoning province. I went there to build a factory for the company I was working for at the time, and Intel was one of my biggest neighbours. Intel's Fab 68, as it is known, first came on line in 2010, and I arrived in 2011. So over my six years living there, I watched an already giant Intel factory grow to truly mega proportions, going through three stages of expansion, each one bigger than the last, with the third stage alone costing $10 billion, and becoming one of Intel's biggest production sites globally.

I was part of a vibrant expat community in Dalian and developed a number of close friendships with people working in the Intel factory there. So it was both interesting and revealing over the years to hear the story of Intel from the insiders' point of view, not just from the massaged, published press releases that every company spits out from time to time. On the surface, Intel looked like a fantastic company, regularly reporting huge record profits and sales growth, with their share price rising from $20 to $55 over this period. But by early 2019, their financial statements started to take a negative turn, with revenue down, operating margin down, earnings per share down – leading to profit warning announcements and less than optimistic trading forecasts for the next three years. Investors started to pull out, affecting the share price as a result. Intel seemed to be falling from its pedestal. And whilst Intel is hardly on its knees right now, this situation has revealed gaps in their strategy, and there is a recognition both within the management and in the investment community that if they don't do something quickly, this downturn could quickly slide further into more negative projections, pushing investors even further away.

The underlying challenge for Intel that is becoming exposed is that for a long time it has been a company focused in two areas, with around 85 percent of its revenue coming from its server data centre and PC Divisions. After several years of trying to diversify, with big announcements, and promises of smart earbuds, smart glasses, smart watches, Intel-driven drones, and even an Intel TV service and self-driving cars, all have failed to materialise or make any credible impact. Its current situation is largely based around Intel's decision in the last ten years to invest heavily in memory chips.

The investment in Dalian Fab 68 was a consequence of this strategy. It was a factory focused on producing memory chips, specifically 3D NAND flash products, mainly for internal consumption in its server data centre and PC Divisions, but with some external sales. Intel placed hefty bets on the rise of memory chips in the market, and started pumping billions into expanding production capacity, as I witnessed in China. But since launching their big investment programme, the NAND flash industry has suffered from oversupply in the market and decreasing prices, and Intel, like other producers, has already said that it will reduce NAND production, with no further additional capacity to be built. The China plant was built in partnership with Micron, and was based on Micron's technology, so the whole situation was not helped by the two companies dissolving their partnership recently.

External sales of 3D NAND products are handled by Intel's NSG (Non-Volatile Memory Solutions Group). But such has been the scale of the investment in the China plant, that even with sales increasing to $4 billion, with the huge depreciation for the plant still on Intel's books, the NSG business has continued to lose big money. The industry is now rife with rumours that Intel's Korean rival, SK Hynix (the world's number two memory chip maker), is going to acquire the Dalian plant in a deal that could wipe out Intel NSG's debt at a stroke.

All of this has brought into sharp focus the apparent inability of Intel as a corporation to successfully diversify. Despite its many attempts to do new things, Intel is still largely the same company it was 30 years ago, a manufacturer of processors and chipsets serving the PC and server markets, whilst the world around it has spawned numerous successful rivals in their market space built around new technologies, like the cloud, that seemed to have passed Intel by. And whilst Intel has been distracted dabbling in new markets over the past ten years, its core PC and server business has come under attack, with competitors like AMD catching up in both chip performance and price, as Intel have been slow in bringing its new miniaturised chip architectures to market. Intel is currently focussing efforts on playing catch up themselves in the growing GPU (graphics processing unit) market, as CPU's move to GPUs for high-performance computing, advanced graphics, and AI computing.

Intel's response to their current situation is they have launched yet another big diversification programme, this one called "Disrupting Intel from the Inside". But how is this going to be different to all the other attempts at diversification that they have tried – and failed at – in the past? I have seen this mistake again and again in businesses I have been involved with. Grand schemes and plans to grow a business, with CEO or presidential announcements to double sales in two or three years, or some such grand goal. All announced in a blaze of glory, with launch events and rousing speeches to rally the troops, and all quickly forgotten about a few months down the road as the pressure of delivering quarterly results takes priority with the executive committee.

But who knows, maybe they have different people involved this time? Maybe they have a new person running the programme? In terms of different people, Intel certainly has a new CEO at the helm now, with the resignation last year of 35-year Intel veteran Brian Krzanich, apparently connected with allegations of violating the company's non-fraternisation policy. But the new CEO, Bob Swan, is likely to be more of the same. Why? Because he is a highly accomplished, career CFO. He is a classic business management professional, who has come up through the functional ranks, and is no doubt extremely competent at executing the current business model. But reference my comments earlier in Chapter 2 ("Why Do Businesses Struggle to Grow through New Products? It All Starts at the Top"). This classic type of leader is incentivised and focused on delivering the numbers, quarter by quarter, and on maximising shareholder value, leading to short term focus and an inevitable struggle to diversify.

So this latest grand "Disrupting Intel from the Inside" diversification initiative runs a serious risk of a whole bunch of hard work by a lot of talented people, that ends up making little impact on Intel's financial performance. Intel have tried many times to move into new markets, with new products, why does the management think this time will be any different? The business can obviously identify new opportunities and have a go at them, they have done it enough times, so finding opportunities, and investing in them, is obviously not their problem. Yet with their new diversification initiative, it appears that they are in danger of just going round the same loop again. When will someone at the top wake up and understand that it is not Intel's ability to identify new opportunities that is the problem, it is their ability to deliver on them. They are a massive corporation and they clearly have the money to make something happen, but they continue to be unsuccessful at innovating in a way that diversifies the business and delivers growth, so there must be something within their business that is holding them back. We are back to those "internal factors" again from Chapter 1 of this book.

Intel's latest efforts could all be in vain if they fail to address in parallel the three fundamental tiers of innovation: if they do not identify and fix those barriers within their own organisation, their innovation process and their culture, that are acting as the bottlenecks to successful new product launches. Instead of launching straight into yet another attempt at diversification, Intel needs to take a good hard look at why they have been unable throughout their history to take their business in a new direction. They need to take a good hard look at what it is about their organisation, about their process and about their culture that is holding back their new technologies and their new products from being successful. Like any of their rivals, they know what's out there in the market, what's up and coming, but they seem unable to do anything meaningful about them. Just launching into another diversification programme runs the risk of repeating the same costly mistakes they have made in the past. Intel have made repeated attempts to diversify and failed every time. Don't they think it is time to stop and ask why? My friends on the inside have told me firsthand that Intel is "just not very good at" exploring new markets. And for senior employees to say that to me, it tells me that there is definitely something ingrained in their business that holds back diversification, almost an expectation of failure. And from my own real-world interactions with some of their staff, Intel appears to be yet another internally focused business, lost in its own world, full of employees speaking their own internal "Intel-ese" language.

Yet Intel is not alone amongst the global mega corporations in its struggle to add profitable, new revenue streams to grow its business over the last 10 to 20 years. Rapid shifts in technology have massively affected many of the markets Intel serves, particularly the move from PCs to mobile devices, which Intel has not only been slow to respond to, but at one point they actively stepped away from the smartphone market during business restructuring activities in 2016, which saw them lay off an incredible 12,000 employees around the globe (11% of their total workforce). A move which caused questions to be asked in the business community about the scale and timeliness of such a massive downsizing, and started a period of intense investor scrutiny.

But why do large corporations like Intel struggle to respond? The list of reasons is a long one: slow decision-making, many layers of management, long communication times and difficult to get the message through, the big corporation leadership mind set of quarterly results and share price, rigid and overly comprehensive business processes, too much central corporate control dictating one size fits all solutions to business divisions, and many more. These all make big corporations slow to respond and too internally focused, which is why almost all the ground-breaking technology and business model innovations have come from the start-up community over the last two decades. With the increasing access the business community now has to venture capital firms, angel investors and other forms of risk capital, the deep pockets of large corporate giants are no longer the only route to investment for clever people with new technology ideas. When I was starting out in business in the late 80s, the normal route to success was bagging a job with a big company and working your way up the corporate ladder. Today, young entrepreneurs can more easily choose to try and make it on their own, given the wide variety of, and ready access to, business support services that are available, and start-ups are launching at a heady rate these days. Indeed, there is quite a culture today taught at business schools and fuelled by government support schemes, which actively encourages young people to start their own business. There are plenty of pluses and minuses to consider regarding taking a business start-up versus a corporate career route, but the situation is now such that anyone with a good idea has the opportunity to explore it without climbing onto a corporate ladder, and this is one of the reasons that big corporations no longer have all the best ideas.

In addition, big companies inevitably focus on and prioritise making the most of their existing products, as these are what pays everyone's salaries and delivers the day-to-day profits. By definition, a start-up does not have that situation, and so all attention becomes focused on innovation, on building a product and a customer base from scratch and on growing the business. The mindset is very different. Plenty of big companies have been trying to find the best of both worlds, by launching innovation initiatives, seeding stand-alone blue skies divisions and incubator centres, all to varied levels of success.

GE's FastWorks programme is a classic modern example of a company-wide innovation initiative that lost its way. Based on Eric Ries' 2011 book *The Lean Startup*, FastWorks was the poster child of such initiatives during the mid-2010's, and an attempt to embed an Agile start-up approach into a large corporation. From 2012 to 2017, FastWorks was rolled out across thousands of senior executives and employed on multiple high-profile product development projects, apparently delivering some great results. But by mid-2017, GE's stock was on a downwards trajectory (it's lost even more value since then, declining 70% within two years), the CEO was gone and FastWorks was at least partly being blamed by investors as a contributing factor, providing too much distraction for the senior team from running the business. This is all in contrast to the golden years of Jack Welch's leadership that I wrote about in Chapter 2. Jack's immediate successor at GE was Jeffrey Immelt, who was CEO from 2001 until his departure in 2017. FastWorks was Immelt's baby, his personal crusade during the second half of his tenure, announced in a blaze of glory just like I wrote about in Chapter 2. FastWorks was his grand announcement, his high-level initiative that was going to take the company to heights hitherto unseen in their business. But why did it seem to fail? He seemed to follow it up personally, and not delegate ownership, just like the successful initiatives I wrote about in Chapter

2 – so what happened? It is certainly debatable whether FastWorks actually failed at all. There were certainly many other factors contributing to GE's downward spiral at the time, but one thing I think we can learn from the FastWorks exercise is that any initiative has to be appropriate. Appropriate to the complexity, to the structure and to the culture of a business. It is difficult to take a one-size-fits-all approach and overlay it onto a business. And it has to be balanced. Grand initiatives are all great starting points, but you have to recognise that people have a day job to do, and they are already busy, so each initiative can, if not controlled carefully and practically, pile more work onto people to see it through. My experience is that success only comes when initiatives are tailored, designed and resourced appropriately to fit a business' needs and capability. That's why I'm not a fan of the headline flag-waving type of initiative. It can be too much of an imposition onto a business – it suggests it hasn't been thought through enough. Another issue I have seen is when initiatives are rolled out every year or two and peter out, then another comes along which peters out, and so on, leading to a credibility issue for top-down initiatives.

From my perspective, what I see as critical in such attempts at trying to create start-ups within big corporations, is achieving the right balance of autonomy versus corporate control, avoiding encumbering such standalone divisions with too much of the corporate culture and their centralised business processes, but also maintaining sufficient links to understand that they are one company and that communication must flow effectively in two directions. I have seen companies that just seem to give such incubators a ton of play money and then don't talk to them for the next year. This is surely a mistake, as any investment needs to maintain a foot in commercial reality if it is to be given any chance at commercial success. The alternative option for many businesses is simply to go out and acquire suitable start-ups that offer potential for their own business. This avoids all the trouble of trying to manage pseudo start-ups yourself but does then have the challenge of integrating the small start-up business effectively into the larger one.

Identifying the "Internal Factors"

I started this chapter with the question "how do businesses get better at innovation?" And I suggested three approaches to gathering the information to help construct a practical way forward. It is important when considering each of the three approaches to understand that every business is unique – your business is unique – and you cannot just take a successful exercise from one company, overlay it onto your own and expect it to succeed. If it was that easy, 89% of businesses would not be struggling to grow. Success is much more subtle and elusive than that, and as we have explored so far in this book, to achieve diversification and growth through innovation and new product development, you first need to put your house in order, in terms of processes, organisation and culture. So in reading case studies and in reviewing your own and others' career experiences, it is important to remember that there are no cut and paste possibilities here, just learning exercises to add data to build the model. The above case study shows how even large companies can struggle with diversification, with implementing grand initiatives and ultimately with trying to grow through new products. So what can you do about it in your business? How can you learn lessons from what has worked and what has not worked in the past and try to apply it successfully to your own business?

We explored the "grand initiatives" approach earlier in Chapter 5, and again in the GE example above. It has always struck me as a very risky approach, not only because it ignores the entire issue of the day-to-day and the innovation sides of your organisation requiring different approaches, but because logically, why would you want to go to the time, trouble and risk to transform your whole business to an Agile (or whatever) one, in the hope that it will speed innovation up for you? It's going to take a long time and absorb a huge amount of your resources, with no guaranteed result, and it's very risky moving everything you do. The classic approach to any improvement process, any root cause analysis, is to look for the rate determining step(s), the main bottlenecks, and focus on eliminating or minimising those. And so the least risky, the fastest and most effective approach to making improvements to your company's ability to grow through new products is to identify those blockers in your organisation, your innovation processes and your culture that are holding you back and deal with them: minimal change, minimal risk, maximum effect.

In reality, there will be much about your business that is already good, some of it will be great. You would not have paying customers if you were not competent at what you do. But every business can improve, and if you are one of the 89% of businesses that is struggling to grow, then you need to first start by recognising that. So how do you identify the good parts versus those parts that are in need of improvement? How do you identify those "internal factors" we discussed at the start of this book? And once you have identified them, what do you do to improve them?

Innovation Auditing

To identify your "internal factors", you need to go through your business with an independent, dispassionate, experienced eye and look at the way your business is organised, what its business processes are and how your people behave and interact. In other words, you need to address the three tiers of innovation, in such a way that you identify what and where are the barriers that are holding back the process of innovation. Essentially, we are talking about doing an audit of your business. Some people don't like the word "audit", it can suggest criticism and some people can get very touchy (this is a reflection on your culture already). So some people talk about it as a maturity assessment or a diagnostic, or some form of due diligence assessment, but call it whatever you want, whatever works for you and your business – though ultimately it is an audit. But where do you start? How do you go about this? Any audit needs some kind of structure to work around, and a process to work through, and this is what I want to address in the rest of this chapter. The structure of the innovation audits I have found to be most effective are built around the three tiers of innovation, which forms the framework as indicated in the graphic below.

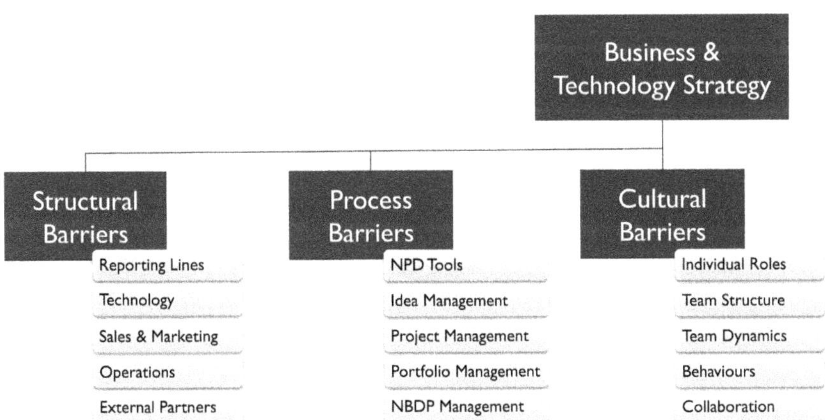

A series of probing questions need to be targeted at key personnel that dig deep into the three tiers, with one set assessing the organisation, looking for structural barriers, one set assessing the innovation process, looking for barriers in the business tools and techniques, and the third investigating the culture, looking for behavioural barriers. In order to maintain context and relevance to the business under scrutiny, all three of these must at all times be interpreted against the backdrop of the business and technology strategy. Another practical thing I have also found in doing these audits, is that it is vital that you have a third party either leading the audit or at least advising you during the audit. It is essential you have someone who is not tainted by what you already think you know about your own business, someone who can cast an experienced eye over what you are doing and tell you like it really is. This is particularly necessary when it comes to working through the cultural part of the audit, because you need someone involved who is not part of the office politics of your own organisation.

Many consulting companies have developed their own checklists and processes to do an innovation audit of a business, and like many other business processes available within the innovation sphere, and plenty of other aspects of running a business, such tools are usually well thought through and well put together, but they almost invariably fall into the bracket of what I call "innovation by numbers". There are tools in the market place, including "house of innovation" and "innovation maturity index" and many others, all marketed as the best of course. But I have seen several of these tools in action at real companies as a customer, and more recently, I have had the chance to interact with people behind the scenes of these businesses, and with practitioners of these tools, and learn how they are taught to run these audits. Many of these consulting companies charge a fee to attend seminars and workshops to teach their "product" to anyone who wants to learn. After only two days of training, anyone can get a license to practise an audit tool. Two days! You can have someone turn up at your company to run an audit who has never managed a business themselves, who has no experience of the complexities and nuances involved, just to run through a "by the numbers" set of questions, and at the end of it they are supposed to advise you on how to do things better. This approach lacks credibility, because as I have repeatedly said in this book, there is no one-size-fits-all approach to innovation, and equally there is no one-size-fits-all approach to innovation auditing. The right set of questions to ask depends heavily on the type of business it is, where it is in its maturity innovation journey, how the business is structured and what its strategy is. Running through a successful audit requires a structured approach, but is almost more of an art form in the way it unfolds and the direction in which it heads, rather than a science. Like any management process, innovation auditing is not a process that anyone can do effectively without a lot of experience. It is easy to run through a standard set of questions and tick all the boxes, and I have seen too many quality audits that are run like this in too many businesses, and I have done this myself in my early career. This is what makes me nervous about the current attempts to build an ISO (International Organization for Standardization) standard around innovation management (ISO 56002:2019). It is fine to want to set some ground rules, I am all for that, that's exactly what I do when I first go into a new business. But setting things like ISO standards can give the illusion, to the uninitiated, that implementing a standard set of innovation processes is all you need to do to get good at innovation. You only need to look at how ISO quality standards are used to understand what I mean.

Plenty of businesses work hard towards achieving ISO-certified quality systems. They put in a comprehensive quality manual, standard operating procedures, a schedule of quality reviews, assign ISO system ownership at each site, and have external auditors come in every year to assess their systems for approval, and all of this is a good thing to have in your business. But in reality, even if your quality system is really good, with well documented procedures, and a good system of regular reviews and updates, and you can proudly display your ISO certification on your website and on your product literature, it does not mean that your products are actually any good. All it means is that you manufacture them consistently and that your supporting business processes are consistent. All good and essential things to have in a business, but just because a business has ISO quality certification in place, it is no reflection on how well their products perform, on the value they bring to their customers. Good quality products only come from setting and working within appropriate technical targets: internally, in terms of manufacturing tolerances, and externally, in terms of delivering performance of value to a customer. In many ways, the ISO quality standards ought to be renamed the ISO consistency standards, because that's the reality of what they reflect. More recent versions of the standard (the current version being ISO 9001:2015) attempt to address this situation by incorporating continuous improvement elements into the standard, but there is only so much you can incorporate into a process, and just like with innovation, quality is really achieved through the skills and professionalism of the management, the technologists, the engineers, the operations teams and the applications team, through collaboration and through leadership. We have seen throughout this book that setting up a process for innovation is just the first step, and that it is the organisation and the culture of a business that make or break a company's ability to grow through new product development.

Prior to launching into an innovation audit, I recommend first that you re-familiarise yourself with the details in my previous book, *Transforming Technology into Profit*, as this will serve as a comprehensive reminder of all the things you should be keeping an eye out for. In particular, I refer you to Chapter 2 of that book, where I wrote about the barriers to "Transforming Technology into Profit", arranged around my 3P's – people, politics and process. These are the things you should aim to unearth during your audit. Following a checklist of questions to find the gaps in a company's innovation process is easy, but having the wisdom and the real-world business experience to see where the real friction lies – between individuals, between teams, between departments – this is where the real value comes from the audit process, because these are the things which are really holding back growth through new products, these are the real "internal factors" at play.

How to Approach an Innovation Audit

Stage 1: Background Information

Any form of innovation audit will start with capturing basic details about an organisation, in order to set context and get a measure of the scale, complexity and reach of the business. A simple spreadsheet is all that is required to capture company name, nature of business, annual turnover, number of employees, number of sites/divisions, market sectors served, geographical markets served, routes to market, key distributors/agents, key customers, etc., along with supporting documents like organisation chart(s), product literature, etc. Much of this basic information is essential not only in building up a picture of the business to provide background for the auditor, but also for the more practical purpose of helping to define the extent of resource and timescale required to complete the audit, as a ten-million-dollar turnover single site is obviously going to be a much quicker assessment than a multi-billion-dollar global company with multiple divisions spread across many time zones. And in fact, some of this fundamental information needs to be captured before the audit even begins, in order to agree resource requirements and timescale, and in order to be able to agree a fee, as auditing is ideally best done by an external expert to provide an unbiased, unblinkered, untainted view of the business. These basic details will also start to shape the approach that the auditor will take, as some questions in their checklist will become less important or irrelevant, whilst others will become essential subjects, requiring more in-depth analysis and more time spent on them. As an external auditor, the company may require you to sign a non-disclosure agreement before starting the audit, as the process may expose you to confidential technology and new product development plans and company strategy, which the company would prefer not to be made public.

Stage 2: Business Strategy

Once the background information has been captured and the audit process has been launched proper, the next stage should focus on understanding the company's business strategy. This is vital in order to allow the auditor to prioritise the rest of the bulk of the audit, as it will indicate what subjects the auditor should focus on, and therefore where to physically spend their time, which may have a significant effect on timescale and costs if lots of flying around the world is required. The split between face-to-face versus virtual, remote interviews that need to be done will be a matter of judgement versus necessity versus budget. During this stage, not only does the auditor need to understand what the business is trying to achieve strategically, they also need to assess how seriously the business takes the strategy and what mechanisms (if any) they have in place to monitor progress. This means drilling down into whether there is a strategy implementation plan in place or whether the business strategy is just words on a PowerPoint presentation; and importantly in terms of innovation, does the business strategy have an associated technology or innovation strategy linked with it, along with metrics and progress review mechanisms. All these things are essential in understanding whether innovation has any chance at all of succeeding within a business. Without such things in place, all efforts towards new product development and commercialisation, however hard people work, run the risk of being misdirected and not contributing to where the business is actually trying to head. As this stage of the audit it is all about getting to grips with the high-level strategic aims of the company, it is important to spend sufficient time with the senior management team, and with the CEO in particular. With any innovation audit, it is important not just to hear everything filtered through the voice of the innovation or technology lead. The person responsible for innovation in a business will have a very different point of view on what is happening in the business compared to many of their colleagues. It is fine for the innovation lead to organise the audit process and to chaperone the auditor, but they should absolutely not be present for much or most of the actual auditing process, as this will skew and contaminate the answers that people give. Leave them out of it as much as possible if you want to get to the truth. Beyond the top team, the auditor will also need to spend time interviewing other key players in the business, to see how the business strategy is cascaded down, to dig down into the reality of how things are actually done on a day-to-day basis with respect to innovation. This can be done during the next stage.

Typical questions you would be asking in this stage are listed below. This is not meant to be an exhaustive list, as additional questions may be needed depending on the nature of the businesses and things that are unearthed during the audit process. As you start interviewing people in the company, there are some basic ground rules that are important to set. One of them is to ask each person to explain what "innovation" means to them. Unless the company has a well communicated definition, then you are very likely to find that innovation means different things to different people in the organisation, and that in itself is a fundamental challenge straight away to building a high performance innovation process in any business. Also, as you start to talk to people, you will need to tailor the terminology you use during your audit into language that is relevant to the particular company you are working with, e.g. do people in the business talk about the technology department or about R&D?

Typical audit questions in Stage 2:

1) Business Strategy
   a. Is innovation or growth from new revenue streams/new product development (NPD) mentioned in your business strategy?

   b. Are there clear guidelines and targets related to this?
   c. Does the strategy explain what things to work on and what not to work on?
   d. How up-to-date and robust do you think your market and competitive data is?
2) Technology (or Innovation) Strategy
   a. Does the company have a clear technology strategy that feeds into the business strategy?
   b. Are there clear guidelines and targets related to this?
   c. Does the strategy explain what things to work on and what not to work on?
3) Senior Management Roles and Accountability
   a. What is the CEO's attitude to innovation/R&D/new product development/new business development? If the CEO doesn't prioritise it, it will not deliver.
   b. Who is responsible for innovation in the senior management team?
   c. Do you have a clear, documented process for innovation?
   d. Who is responsible for R&D? Are R&D, new product development and new business development managed separately?
   e. Who is responsible for commercialising new products?
   f. Who is responsible for IP? Who manages your IP portfolio? Is IP part of the technical function or the commercial function?
   g. How many patents do you have? Are you getting value out of these patents?
   h. Who is responsible for delivering new products and adding new revenue streams to the business? Is this all focused on the R&D department or spread between functions?
   i. Is innovation/new product development/new business development a clear agenda item at each executive or board meeting? - If not, then it will never get the priority it needs to deliver.
4) Innovation/R&D/New Product Development/New Business Development Project Portfolio
   a. What innovation/R&D/new product development/new business development metrics are in place?
   b. How many innovation/R&D/new product development/new business development projects are currently live?

c. What is your innovation/R&D/new product development/new business development budget?
d. What is your innovation/R&D/new product development/new business development projected sales delivery?
e. How many innovation/R&D/new product development/new business development projects did you kill in the last 12 months?
f. What is the percentage of new products sales, annual trend and target?
g. What is your company's definition of a new product?

Stage 3: Structural Barriers

Once you have talked to the senior management, you will need to dig into the organisation and start talking to the rest of the company staff, particularly the functional heads, partly to see if they have the same view as the senior management, but also to understand the details, which the senior team are unlikely to know. Stage 3 is all about trying to identify the key functional interfaces that exist within the organisation and to assess whether they are well understood and being managed effectively, or at all.

Typical audit questions in Stage 3:

1) Structural Barriers – with reference to the company innovation process:
    a. Describe the business structure and reporting hierarchy.
    b. How does the R&D team interact with the rest of the organisation? Do we have an ivory tower?
    c. How does the R&D team interact with customers?
    d. What percentage of the R&D department's time is spent on developing new products versus supporting existing products (e.g. 30% new products versus 70% existing products)?
    e. How are the sales team incentivised with respect to new product sales?
    f. How do the technology and sales and marketing functions interact? Any shared responsibilities (looking for silos and any ambiguity or lack of clear responsibilities)?
    g. How do the technology and operations functions interact? Any shared responsibilities (looking for silos and any ambiguity or lack of clear responsibilities)?

h. How do the sales and marketing and operations functions interact? Any shared responsibilities (looking for silos and any ambiguity or lack of clear responsibilities)?
i. What skills do you lack in-house that you outsource or partner externally for?
j. What external partners are involved in your innovation portfolio? Are they trying to do too much themselves in-house?
k. Where do application engineering roles report into?

Stage 4: Process Barriers

Stage 4 is all about investigating what tools and techniques are in place to manage the process of innovation, from how the company generates and captures ideas, what process they use to assess and prioritise these ideas, through to the management and implementation of projects and commercialisation of new products. Refer back to the summary of the process in Chapter 1 for a full list of what is involved. This is where you assess how sophisticated the business is in terms of managing the whole of the innovation funnel and how well joined up the processes are. Is there anything missing? Are the tools as efficient and as suitable as possible for the business? Here, the innovation lead themselves will certainly be able to give you the company stance on what the innovation process is (if they have one), but it is only by interviewing other staff, particularly those that ought to be involved in it, that you can actually get to see the reality of whether the process is really adhered to on a practical basis. What can be really useful in this stage is to go through an example of a real project with one of the staff, getting them to walk you through each stage of the process steps it went through. In this way you can assess for yourself the tools used and how all the files are documented on the company's server, including how they are accessed and by whom.

Typical audit questions in Stage 4:

1) Idea Management
   a. Describe the process and techniques used to generate ideas for new products.
   b. Do you run brainstorming events or technology roadmapping events? How are these managed?

   c. Describe the process used to manage new product ideas, after they are generated.
   d. Describe the process used to select and prioritise ideas for new products.
   e. How do you decide which ideas to fund and transform into projects?
2) R&D and New Business Project Management
   a. How do you budget for innovation/R&D/new product development/new business development projects?
   b. What project management systems do you use (e.g. phase-gate, Agile, etc)?
      i. How do you manage R&D projects?
      ii. How do you manage scale-up of new technologies and products?
      iii. How do you manage productionisation? Who is involved?
      iv. How do you manage new product launch? Who is involved?
   c. How do you manage the full portfolio of projects? How do you decide which projects are higher priority?
3) Commercialisation
   a. Do you do a post-implementation project review?
   b. How do you manage the new business development pipeline?
4) Overview of process
   a. How easy are the above tools/processes to use?
   b. Are there too many tools and/or too complex? How long do they take to administer?
   c. Are your tools largely spreadsheet or software driven?
   d. How comprehensively do people complete/use the tools/processes in place?

Stage 5: Cultural Barriers

Stage 5 is the most difficult one to do right. Whilst much of the previous stages involves information gathering, stage 5 requires the auditor to delve into those touchy-feely subjects of team dynamics, and behavioural aspects of collaboration and how people interact with respect to the innovation process. This is where you need to be looking out for the people and politics aspects of the barriers to "transforming technology into profit", mentioned earlier. To do this stage effectively, you need to spend time sitting in on meetings to really watch how key people interact. The type of person who can do stage 5 best is often a different type of person to that who can do the previous four stages well, due to the nature of the interpersonal skills approach involved, and so it may be best, if budget allows, to bring in a specialist for stage 5, to support the lead auditor, and ensure the audit is done as well as possible. Indeed, as stage 5 is the most difficult of all to get right, the unfortunate reality is that many auditors will gloss over it, or run out of time, as they prioritised the earlier items that they are more comfortable with, or indeed miss it out altogether.

Typical Audit Questions in Stage 5:

1) Team Dynamics
   a. How much of your time is spent in internal meetings?
   b. How much of your time is spent interacting with customers? Is there too much internal focus in the business?
   c. At meetings, are team roles clear?
   d. Are meetings run with a clear purpose, agenda, timekeeping, and chaired effectively?
   e. Are meeting actions recorded effectively and followed up rigorously?
2) Key Skills
   a. Who are the individuals that are good at generating ideas?
   b. Who are the individuals that are good at implementing ideas?
3) Culture Overview
   a. How would you describe the culture of innovation within your business?
   b. How would you describe the culture of collaboration within your business?
   c. How do non-technical people view the technical people? What are the words they use? Any "nerds" or "geeks" words used (indicates culture and stigma issues)?
   d. Is there any jargon regularly used within your business that confuses you?
   e. What aspects of people's behaviour/language in relation to encouraging innovation do you like/dislike?
   f. Any idea killers in your organisation? Anybody use the phrase "We tried that before and it didn't work"?

g. For multi-site businesses – Have you experienced "not invented here syndrome" within your business?

Gap Analysis

If you're struggling to make sense of some of the vague answers you get during your audit, one useful technique you can employ during an audit to get some measure of the more intangible things you are trying to investigate, is to do a gap analysis. Typically, this means getting the person to rate the subject on a scale of one to ten (one being the worst, ten being the best). This is best done with concepts like innovation and collaboration, because if you ask a person to describe how good these things are in a business, then you will only get subjective "good or bad" type answers, terms which are relative in meaning depending on the person's point of view. You can also usefully use this gap analysis approach in meetings or workshops when preparing for the audit with the management team, or afterwards, in a workshop to lay the foundations for a new approach to innovation in their business. Typical questions you might use this approach with during an innovation audit include:

1) How innovative do you think your company is? (This rating will typically vary a lot when you ask different individuals in a business, reflecting the wide variety of attitudes people have towards it.)
2) How innovative do you think the people in your company are? (This answer will always be higher than the previous question, as people invariably think that there are some really talented people in their business, but that the company does not make the most of their talent. This is a great opener to start discussing why the difference between the two ratings.)
3) How innovative do you think your company needs to be?
4) How collaborative do you think your people are?
5) How collaborative do you think your people need to be?
6) How much training do you receive in relation to creating a culture of collaboration and innovation?

Given the number of stages required to complete a comprehensive innovation audit, and the many questions you need to ask, you can see that an audit can be quite a lengthy process, requiring significant time and resources, not only from the auditor but also from the many individuals that will need to be part of the assessment procedure. It takes a lot of commitment to complete. And it's no good trying to cut it short and do only part of the audit, because you are likely to miss the most important barriers that are holding back successful innovation and growth for your business. Since successful innovation is a fully holistic activity, not just a complex process, requiring all three of the tiers of successful innovation to make it work, then it would be foolish to do anything less than the complete audit process.

7

UNLOCKING YOUR GROWTH POTENTIAL

> My academic background is science so when I began my career over 20 years ago and quickly moved to leadership roles, I had a lot to learn about becoming a people leader (and still do…)
>
> Phil Clark, Global Technical Director, Automotive and Aerospace Division at 3M

How Do Businesses Get Better at Innovation?

So, you've done the audit, you've identified the barriers, and you've written a report. So what next? What do you do with all the information you have generated? Your audit will have generated a lot of information, it will have highlighted several gaps in the process, some areas of concern in the way the structural interfaces are managed and maybe some issues with collaboration and team dynamics. There are always many things that can be put right in any company's ability to innovate and grow through new products, no company is perfect. One likely outcome is that there will be too many things to deal with all at once, but do you really need to put them all right?

Once you have formulated your conclusions, you need to review them with the senior management team of the company. Your initial review may highlight a few things you misinterpreted, or key information you did not pick up on, which skewed your findings, things which might require you to go back and talk to a few more people. Whether this happens or not, it is essential that you discuss your conclusions openly with the management team, in a non-biased, non-judgemental, professional manner, and then reach agreement. The team has to buy in to what you are saying, otherwise it will affect the quality and effectiveness of the follow-up. Of the many findings, you also need to mutually agree on priorities by asking such questions as: which are the most glaring gaps in their innovation process? Where is there the biggest internal communication problem between departments? What are the biggest behavioural barriers? Here you will need to use your skill, experience and judgement to identity those items on your list that are having the biggest effect on slowing down the business' ability to come up with new ideas and turn them into profitable new products in the market. Some of the things you identify in the business will be having a much bigger influence on this than others, will be much bigger barriers, and it is these that need to be put right first. Congratulations, you have finally identified those "internal factors" that we talked about right at the beginning of this book, in Chapter 1.

The next important step is to prepare and agree on an action plan with the senior management team. Some of the "internal factors" may have straightforward solutions, whilst some of them are going to require a lot of hard work to deal with. So depending on what factors you have identified and agreed, there should hopefully be some low-hanging fruit that you can focus in on to get some quick wins, but also there will be some underlying, fundamental challenges that need to be dealt with. At this stage, as you put the action plan together, the company may decide that your role as innovation auditor is over and from this point onwards it is an internal matter to be dealt with by the company. That is fine, and that is their decision. But typically what I have found is that in reviewing the opportunities for improvement, and in putting together the plan, there will be some items that are naturally better dealt with by the company themselves, these are usually structural things, like changing reporting lines, whilst there are other types of things that are best done by an external partner. These are typically behavioural and cultural matters, and are always best done by an external, independent support person, because if a company is working to improve team dynamics, collaboration and behavioural matters, then it is much better to have someone leading that who is completely outside of the organisation, someone who is not part of the day-to-day office politics. Any process barriers identified are typically handled with a combination of internal resource and external support, depending on what process, tools or techniques need putting in place. A typical example of how action planning is distributed between internal versus external resources is shown below.

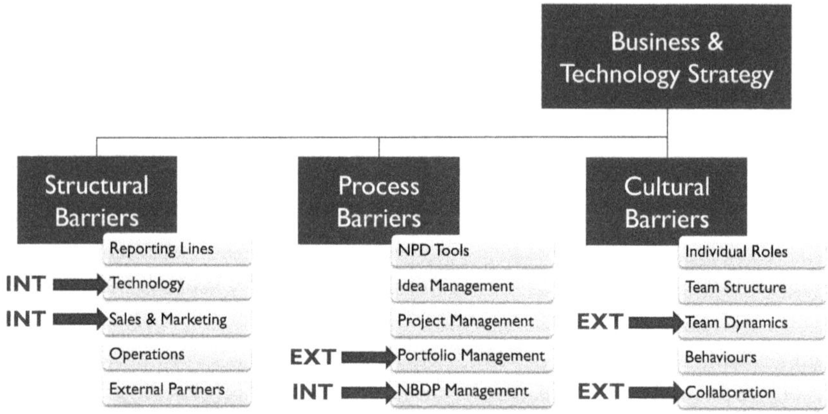

Regular follow-up and progress review on the action plan is very important, to avoid loss of momentum on making the changes. This should be treated as a project, and managed with the same discipline and project management approach that any major project in a business would be dealt with. This will require at least monthly reviews, and depending on the scale and complexity of the things you have chosen to work on, the project may continue for at least one year, possibly two. A rigorous approach to implementation is what is needed to make a real difference to the business. Further downstream, the results of what is achieved through the action plan, should be monitored with all those KPIs that measure growth and new product sales in the business. This is what will ultimately prove if you have all done your job correctly.

Getting Better at People Management

During my own career, I have found myself leading a wide variety of business functions, from innovation and product development, operations and quality, to P&L ownership and construction projects, and whilst they all require their own specialist technical skills to succeed, I have certainly found that there is a common set of managerial and leadership skills required whatever the functional role. And so, when it comes to "transforming technology into profit", not only do you need to develop the specialist skills discussed in this book, you also need to become a better manager, both of yourself and of other people. You cannot achieve success in any aspect of business without this. As we have explored throughout this book, as early as Chapter 1, the three tiers of successful innovation – structure, process and culture – all revolve around people, so without developing people skills you are never going to be able to successfully manage the functional interfaces of an organisation, never going to get the buy-in of your team members and of other managers into your innovation business process, and you're never going to be able to navigate the subtle interactions of team dynamics and coach people on appropriate behaviours.

One senior executive that shares these views is Phil Clark. Phil is Global Technical Director of 3M's Automotive and Aerospace Solutions Division and has been working in technology leadership roles for over 20 years. 3M is a $33 billion multinational corporation, operating in more than 70 countries, with over 93,000 employees. 3M has built a very strong reputation as an innovator in industry, worker safety, health care, and consumer goods, not least because it produces a vast array of over 60,000 products, including many well-known brands, and is frequently held up as a leader in the field of new product development.

From his earliest days starting out in his industrial career, following his academic studies at Harvard University, Phil recognised that having an academic background in science in no way prepared him for the business leadership roles in which he found himself, and so began a career-long and continuous passion for learning how to become a better people leader. In relation to leading technology and innovation, Phil categorises his approach into three levels: 1) Individuals – how to further develop himself and work better with others, 2) Teams – how to better manage teams and get team members to work better together and 3) Culture – how to develop the right working culture to support innovation, create new products and deliver business growth.

Individuals – The Challenges

When it comes to individual people management, whether of self or others, Phil has identified several key challenges that can affect his day-to-day role:

1) Cultural differences – as a global company, 3M works with people all over the world, so Phil is constantly aware of the cultural differences that need to be considered when interacting with individuals from different countries and across continents. And it's not just an issue of relevance to people from different countries: in his current role, Phil is based in the US, in Minneapolis, but originally hails from Boston, and even recognises subtle differences in working style between people from the East Coast versus the Midwest of the US, most notably in things like the levels of candour and openness that people display.
2) Training backgrounds – Phil's formal academic training was in the natural sciences, in basic scientific subjects, but in his current role he finds himself working a lot with engineers, who because of their different training and background, approach things in a different way, use different vocabulary and display different views of things.
3) Employment experience – Phil has observed that a person's employment history can have a profound effect on the working culture that an individual brings with them to 3M. For example, there can be a big difference in attitude between those hired mid-career from another company versus new hires straight out of university, and between those who have worked at multiple companies and been exposed to different working cultures, versus those who have only ever worked in one business. In addition, the current trend towards a more mobile workforce brings with it yet another set of working attitudes. This highlights that business culture is set not only from the top down, by the words and deeds of the leadership team, but also from the bottom up, by the experiences and attitudes that employees bring with them into the business.
4) Individual motivation and preferences – managing different personality types is a challenge for all managers, compounded by the fact that some people prefer to work alone, whereas others prefer to work in teams.

Individuals – The Solutions

Just as the challenges of individual people management are many and varied, so they need to be tackled with a variety of methods. And not only that, such approaches and working techniques need to become incorporated into everyone's day-to-day operating rhythm. Developing emotional intelligence (EQ) is like developing a muscle: if you don't use it regularly, it will atrophy.

1) Understanding personality types – managing different personalities is a challenge for all managers, and Phil has tried a variety of tools over the years to assist him. One method he has found works well in the 3M environment is based upon Tom Rath's book *StrengthsFinder 2.0*. The book is structured such that you read a short section about "finding your strengths" and then take an online assessment, where upon you receive a detailed report on your "five themes", highlighting your key strengths, along with strategies on how best to apply them. There are many other personality analysis tools available, and whatever method you find works for you and your business environment, using a common tool throughout your group helps to establish a common vocabulary with which to articulate individual strengths and how they can complement one another. Phil was convinced by the StrengthsFinder approach when it resolved issues with a colleague he worked with some years ago. Although they respected each other, their communication was not always productive. To try to improve, they decided to share their StrengthsFinder 2.0 assessments with each other. This resulted in several "aha!" moments that fundamentally improved the productiveness of their communication. The sharing of their personality assessments essentially created an opportunity for them to explore each other's strengths and perspective in an open and non-judgemental way. Phil has since found this approach to be a great way to get to know his team better and for them to get to know him.
2) Ata-bench – Phil described to me how he initiated an interesting programme within the divisions he has led at 3M that has proved very effective at breaking down the "us and them" barrier between management and employees. "Ata-bench" enables him to spend half a day per month working at the laboratory bench alongside his technical

team, working on the same practical tasks, but without the managerial label. Not only has this proven useful in building respect from the team, but Phil has personally found it helpful in sharpening and refreshing his own technical skills. In addition, as it gives exposure to the day-to-day practical challenges facing the team, Phil can see more clearly why requests for new equipment and resources are made, speeding up decision-making for large spend items.

3) Reverse mentor – during his 3M career, Phil found himself working increasingly with engineers, but since he didn't have an engineering background himself, he found it a struggle to accommodate their approach to work and to get the best out of working relationships. He tackled this head on by finding someone in his organisation who was willing to teach him about Chemical Engineering and together they began a series of regular one-on-one meetings. 3M does have its own in-house technical education, so Phil could have gone to learn about the subject himself, but working one-on-one with his "reverse mentor" had significant additional benefits that he just couldn't have got through the self-teaching route. In particular, his teacher was a researcher three tiers down in the organisation, and so the relationship helped to break down management layers, and also, by opening himself up in this way and working with a junior engineer, it also displayed vulnerability and broadcast his accessibility.
4) 3M internal development programmes – in addition to Phil's own approaches to self-improvement and getting better at working with and managing individuals, 3M also has in place a number of formal internal development programmes. These may include leadership training programmes, three-to-five-day immersion training, and a six-week business school online course, which together provide a comprehensive and common approach. Aside from the formal training, Phil also recognises the importance and value of the informal opportunities that working in a multinational corporation brings that work towards breaking down barriers, finding common ground and building better working relationships. Simply taking the opportunity to share personal interests with colleagues, and getting to know them beyond their workplace façade, can make big strides in relationship building. And in terms of building self-confidence and personal resilience, Phil also talks about the value of "getting comfortable being

uncomfortable" and cites the international travel opportunities that working in a global business brings as one of the practical ways of achieving this.

Teams – The Challenges

When working with groups, Phil has identified several challenges that can affect team performance with respect to the technology and innovation function:

1) "You can't schedule innovation" – there can be an attitude from some members of technology teams that the development of new technologies and new products are processes that have to be left to progress naturally, nurtured by expert proponents in the field. And because there is no guarantee that any particular avenue of development is going to deliver what was targeted, when it comes to the discipline of project planning, setting milestones, and agreeing delivery dates, such individuals argue that "you can't schedule innovation".
2) Non-value-added processes – Phil also occasionally encounters the view in project teams that some of the internal innovation processes used by corporations are non-value-adding, and take up too much time away from the bench. In a similar vein, internal demands from management are also sometimes seen as a hindrance to innovation rather than a help.
3) Lack of customer centricity – Phil has observed in some project team scenarios that they can become very insular, and too focused on the technical task in hand. This has the negative effect that the team can lose sight of the customer, and the very reason they are working on the task in the first place, with the very real risk of project drift.

Teams – The Solutions

Phil has explored several approaches with his teams:

1) Scheduling tools – to deal with the "you can't schedule innovation" issue, Phil has recently been working with OKRs (objectives and key results) as an alternative to traditional Gantt charts and their

associated KPIs (key performance indicators). The OKR approach to project management originally came out of Intel in the 70s. Google was an early adopter, and some cite OKRs as a major contributor to their meteoric success. The approach was subsequently picked up by many other software-based companies (LinkedIn, Twitter, Uber, Netflix, Amazon, Dropbox, etc.). The industrial project management discipline of phase-gate (see Chapter 1) is normally driven through the gates using timescale and milestone planning tools like Gantt charts, coupled with quantitative targets and performance metrics in the form of KPIs, which together act as a monitor of progress towards the project goals. OKRs offer an alternative approach to goal setting and progress measurement, in that the method does not strive for 100% success, and deliberately sets qualitative, ambitious goals which are slightly beyond the reach of the team, with progress measured as a percentage grading against the goals. The benefit of this approach for a team is a motivational one, as there is no simple pass/fail against a target (70% achievement is still considered good progress), which in turn builds recognition that their performance can be further improved. As with all business processes, it is about selecting the right tool for the job, and the Gantt/KPI and OKR approaches both have their place as project management tools. The defined timescales and hard targets of the Gantt/KPI approach is generally most appropriate if your task is to deliver something tangible and specific, like a generation 2 evolution of a product. On the other hand, the stretched goals and flexibility in planning that OKRs offer may be more appropriate if you have a grander, more aggressive objective or are looking to change strategic direction in a business and want to gain alignment throughout the entire organisation.

2) Innovation processes – like many industrial companies, 3M have been using a well-developed and mature phase-gate process for managing product development projects. The standard company-wide process was built around seven phases, each having a phase gate. But it is also recognised that different divisions within the business serve different markets and those markets have different requirements. And so, whilst there had been a standardised phase-gate process, 3M has now moved to a new commercialisation system that is divided into two sections: Discover and phase gate. The Discover phase is flexible and

tailorable to a particular division's needs. The phase-gate process may be reduced to three Phases each having a phase gate and starts once the business case, including technical feasibility, has been demonstrated and approved. It is not a completely rigid system. For example, Phil's business serves the automotive and aerospace markets, which are both highly regulated sectors, and so needs a highly structured and disciplined approach to project management, therefore within the Discover phase, Phil has implemented two phases with formal reviews.

3) Customer focus – phase-gate processes ensure that the customer is maintained as a consistent priority during the whole of the innovation process. When it comes to taking new products to market, commercialising new products into existing markets or adjacent markets are treated very differently, as a product line extension into an existing market has a different level of commercial risk compared to a brand-new product in a brand-new market. In an attempt to introduce a "move fast" mentality into the commercialisation phase of projects, 3M is currently exploring the introduction of elements of Agile project management (see Chapter 3) through the use of a scrum-style environment for the commercialisation team, with activities based around sprints, as with the classic software development methodology.

Culture, Structure and People Management

When it comes to culture, leaders can have several initiatives in place to ensure the right behaviours are constantly reinforced, and maintain a reporting structure that facilitates collaboration, such that the organisation heads in the right direction and people continue to contribute to rather than detract from the goal of delivering new products.

1) Leadership behaviours – for example, 3M widely publicise a set of leadership behaviours throughout their organisation. These are designed to provide clear guidelines for how every person in the company should aspire to conduct themselves. The six behaviours are: 1) play to win, 2) foster collaboration and teamwork, 3) prioritise and execute, 4) develop others and self, 5) innovate, 6) act with integrity and

transparency. These behaviours are constantly reinforced throughout the business, including posters hanging in 3M offices all over the world. Leadership behaviours have been a part of 3M culture for the last fifteen years and are intimately woven into the annual performance review system, with individuals scored once a year on a 1–5 basis. The value of this is that it is a conversation opener about how people are perceived and can lead into coaching opportunities.

2) Organisational structure – each product portfolio needs to have a clear leadership pairing of a technical and a business manager. Sales management tends to be geographically focused, offering cross-platform support. All three come together when it comes to commercialisation of new products, and this is considered a critical focal point for cross-functional collaboration requiring formal management. Individuals get assigned to formal commercialisation teams to avoid ambiguity of priorities, allowing people the freedom to work at the functional interfaces that are so important to making innovation a success. There has grown a real kudos around being involved in these teams, with formal team awards presented for hitting targets and highly sought-after personal recognition awards that winners proudly display on their desks.
3) Communication – in order to ensure everyone is up to date with progress made by the cross-functional commercialisation teams, many divisions publish quarterly highlights, which include customer-based success stories and financial performance from new products (defined as a product launched in the last five years), broken down by product platform. For example, to ensure comprehensive coverage at 3M, each active new product programme will have its own page in the quarterly highlights and there will typically be between 50 and 100 such programmes per division. Communication goes two-way in 3M, with regular employee surveys to gauge attitudes on a number of topics in the business.

After my discussions with Phil, the overall impression I am left with of his leadership is that it is part of a well embedded innovation process, supported by a strong culture of personal development and a well-structured organisation that actively tries to optimise collaboration. I know from my own experience that achieving all of this in such a massive global organisation is no mean feat, and certainly doesn't happen by accident. I know the hard work and strategic thinking that has to go into successfully managing structure, process and culture, and after hearing Phil's experience of working in such an environment, it is now much clearer to me why 3M is so frequently held up as the ultimate new product development machine.

Getting Better at Innovation Strategy

Throughout this and my previous book, *Transforming Technology into Profit*, I frequently refer to the importance of having a business strategy, against which to hold up all the plans and actions you want to implement within the business. A good strategy should give clear direction and a set of practical guidelines that give context to everything you do, to ensure that all activities are contributing positively to the business and heading in the same direction. And the strategy also needs to be interpreted in the shape of a supporting innovation strategy, which will clarify what things you must be doing within the technology and associated functions to play their part in delivering the overall business strategy. However, we have yet to explore what that truly looks like, so what better way, as we come towards the conclusion of this book, to go right back to the beginning and to explore what this really means and what a good strategy should look like. And what better way to dig into this topic than to explore the innovation strategy of one of the biggest industrial companies on the planet, DuPont.

My conversation with Alexa Dembek, Chief Technology and Sustainability Officer (CTSO) at DuPont was very timely, as she was busy preparing for an innovation strategy review at the next DuPont board meeting the following month, so this subject was front and centre in her mind. DuPont is a US-based conglomerate, founded in 1802, renowned for introducing numerous new materials over its long history, including well-known brands and materials such as Teflon, nylon, Kevlar®, Tyvek® and Lycra. In 2017 the company merged with Dow Chemical to create DowDuPont, the world's largest chemical company, which subsequently spun off three businesses, one of which is the new DuPont.

Alexa is a 28-year veteran of DuPont. Today, she leads business and innovation strategy alignment to make the most impactful portfolio choices for DuPont. Her goal is to make every investment dollar count to quickly drive innovation to market. She is passionate about elevating the role sustainability plays in these investment decisions and how DuPont can help customers achieve their own sustainability ambitions with DuPont solutions.

Given its recent merger and reorganisation, even though it's 218 years old, Alexa says she sees today's DuPont as a brand-new company. The mindset is that of a 218-year-old start up, but one that uniquely possess the institutional knowledge of a long history and powerful legacy of scientific innovation. And because of the recent structural changes following the merger, Alexa very much sees her role as building this bridge between the past, present and future to ensure DuPont's long-term relevancy for today's dynamic markets and global challenges.

From this reference point, at DuPont, innovation is synonymous with growth. It is considered to be a key financial lever to drive growth for the company. Innovation is viewed holistically throughout the business as having four key components: 1) new products, 2) new applications, 3) new processes and 4) new business models. Innovation is not just thought of as R&D (though R&D is a key enabler), it is not considered a department, it is pivotal to everyone's role in driving success, whether in the lab or on the marketing team – everyone is responsible.

DuPont's strategy is focused on looking deeply into their markets to identify the important customer needs, seeking out problems which are both important and valuable to solve. To capture these opportunities, there is a recognition that the business will need to continuously adjust and evolve its in-house capabilities, and develop external partnerships to access key capabilities, and that going forward, there will be no such thing as "business as usual".

In order to support the delivery of this strategy, Alexa sees three particular priorities for her role: 1) accountability with the business presidents to the CEO for $900 million investment in R&D, 2) a need to focus on speed to achieve higher returns, faster, and 3) building an expectation that at DuPont they will be perpetually driving innovation, that it will never stop.

When it comes to the need to increase the speed and impact of innovation to drive growth, Alexa recognises that scale is a complicating factor. Achieving this in a $1 billion organisation is hard enough, but it's even harder at $22 billion, DuPont's current turnover since the spin-off. Some of the other big challenges that Alexa sees in delivering on her role include how to foster the mindset for innovation and how to increase early stage innovation. DuPont is a very technology- and science-rich community, but it is recognised that opportunities cannot start in a laboratory and that incremental innovation is not good enough anymore as it is not delivering enough growth. To deliver on the desire for speed, Alexa is reorienting the business' focus externally, to better understand customer value and industry dynamics and to open up external partnerships. In this way, she believes the business will be in a better position to make choices about what they work on, to change the way they balance the project portfolio and to better enable additional future capabilities.

Culturally, like many businesses, "not invented here syndrome" was strong in DuPont ten to twenty years ago, and it was widely recognised that the business had to work to move away from that situation to become the more entrepreneurial environment it is today. There are three behaviours that DuPont has encouraged in all of its employees to achieve this shift: 1) make an impact, 2) act as an owner, 3) partner with customers. The leadership team understands that trying to achieve a behavioural shift cannot be done by just running a project, and that these principles need to be constantly reinforced on a day-to-day basis in order to bring them to life.

DuPont's stated mission is to, "empower the world with the essential innovations to thrive", but the leadership recognises that this is not going to be delivered just with good science, it also has to be done with technology that adds value to customers. And in terms of innovation underpinning DuPont's strategy, it's not just about technology. There is a key message in Alexa's job title, not just Chief Technology Officer, but Chief Technology and Sustainability Officer. This sends a clear message to their customers and employees about what Dupont wants to prioritise and promote, with a key focus on sustainable innovations, such as electric vehicles, next generation healthy foods and probiotics. Alexa firmly believes that innovation and sustainability are two sides of the same coin: "our innovation strategy is aligned with the significant challenges highlighted in the United Nations' Sustainable Development Goals, such as providing solutions to mitigate climate change, delivering technologies to support life-saving health care and helping to make drinking water safer and more accessible". But also, that with the increasing pressure on many topics, such as single-use plastics, given the changes in behaviours that these are driving into the future, innovation for sustainability is also aligned with value creation.

So What Can You Do Differently?

My advice to everyone struggling with the challenge of developing and commercialising new products in a business, especially those younger innovators out there in corporate land, who are still early on in their innovation journey, is: if you want your new product to succeed, then don't focus as most people do solely and exhaustively on improving your processes, think also about how your process fits into the whole three-tier scheme of innovation. It may not be what you are doing that is holding back your next great new product, the barriers are more likely to be hidden somewhere in the way that your organisation is structured and the attitudes and behaviours of key individuals in the business.

Just doing great technology is not enough today to guarantee success. There are many gifted technologists working in industry today, doing some really clever stuff. And focussing on improving your innovation processes is also not enough today, despite what all those companies out there trying to sell you their project management and innovation software claim. To truly succeed in "transforming technology into profit", you have to understand that your project has to happen within an existing business, with lots of different people, with many complex relationships, and all the baggage that those inevitably bring. These are the true challenges that you have to learn to deal with in commercialising any technology, and these are the things they don't teach you when you are learning about science and technology at college or university.

When you are learning your technical trade, slowly becoming an expert in some particular branch of chemistry, physics, engineering, biochemistry or whatever, your degree or postgrad course successfully teaches you enough technical skills to put you on a path of technical creativity and lifelong learning in your field, giving you a great foundation in technical expertise from which to build a career in technical innovation and new product development. And so when you move on from academia and get a job in industry, it is easy to think you have all the skills you need to develop some wonderful new products. I certainly felt empowered in the early years of my career to be highly innovative and create lots of new things for the business within which I worked. But what a frustrating experience it turned out to be once the reality hit home that my PhD and my technical prowess weren't enough on their own to deliver new products out into the world. No one explained this to me, no one warned me, and I don't think back in those days anyone really understood the subtleties of how to make technology work for a business. Some people were just good at it, the rest of us had to learn the hard way. This book is the story of how and what I learnt. Slowly unfolding over the many chapters, until hopefully you have a better appreciation of how new product ideas can be managed carefully through the many barriers and out to customers.

To be successful with developing and commercialising new products, you have to look for the barriers and gaps in your own business that are holding back successful exploitation of new technology, maybe it's in the organisation, in the culture or in the processes. Seek out those barriers and work to deal with them. In this way you will unlock the potential of your business and deliver better, more profitable new products faster to your customers. To draw a close to the main body of this book, I thought a short summary of the key themes would prove useful:

1) Put in the right innovation processes for your business – you don't need all the latest, all singing, all dancing, ultra-comprehensive tools to run an effective innovation process. You just need the appropriate ones for the size and scale of your business and for the diversity and subtlety of the markets you serve. Simplicity is key, don't overcomplicate data capture, data management and data review, it will draw you and your organisation into too much internal focus and cause you to drift away from your customers.
2) Optimising organisational structure – setting structure and a reporting hierarchy is a powerful way of forcing the right interactions, to get the right people together in the right forums to work effectively together. This isn't going to happen if your business is structured in classic departmentalised silos. A classic challenge in any medium to large company is achieving the right balance of internally focused versus externally focused structure. Many businesses naturally develop with an internal focus. Departments and subsidiary groups of companies tend to be built around the technologies they are built upon, rather than grouped around the markets they serve, even if their website and literature says otherwise. Outwardly, many companies present themselves as having an automotive division or a construction division or an energy division, but internally their organisation is grouped around

the technologies that are used to create the products to serve these industries. So you might get a company in the US that manufactures elastomeric polymers, grouped together in a division with another elastomeric polymer producer in Europe and another with a similar producer in Asia. Why? Because internally there are organisational benchmarking benefits to be had. These companies are likely buying similar feedstock, so there are bulk purchasing deals to be done. These companies likely share manufacturing processes, so there are operational benchmarking savings and efficiencies to be had by working together to determine best practice. You can see why internally focused companies have benefits, but they are all internal benefits, they rarely help the customer. But the reality is that each company is serving multiple markets with their elastomeric polymer technology, usually some similar markets, though often not identical. So the US firm might be serving the automotive and construction markets, the European plant might be serving the construction and energy markets, and the Asian site might be serving the automotive and energy markets. So it doesn't naturally fall into place that these separate businesses can work together cohesively as a one-market-facing entity. So you can see how things start to get complicated. These types of organisational structure are a natural consequence of business growth and acquisition, but sooner or later businesses realise that they would be better organised in a market-facing structure to focus outwardly on customers, rather than inwardly on technologies. But by then it is invariably extremely difficult to unpick a structure that is usually decades old, in some cases even longer. The ways of working and the groupings that the employees are used to working in, the relationships they have built, are all based around the internal focus of the organisational structure. And that is a huge task to attempt to unpick. That's where transformational change programmes are necessary to plan and guide businesses down a different path. Yet, when businesses attempt to go that way, they find themselves in another, equally challenging non-ideal situation. So a business goes through the upheaval of creating an automotive division, it goes through all the people throwing their toys out of the pram, etc. It then discovers that automotive is actually a huge supply chain with multiple entry points, multiple tiers, and the different companies and teams you have pulled together don't actually talk to the same customers, or about the same application anyway, so where was the synergy? Brave companies go one step towards this by splitting manufacturing from sales, and keep the manufacturing sites inwardly structured and the sales teams outwardly structured. It makes sense, but it's a big management challenge to maintain some sense of cohesion around the company culture when there is this huge gap between two big silos you have created. The reality I have discovered in my own career is that true synergistic groupings that serve both your business and a customer's business is not around technologies, or around markets, it is actually somewhere in the middle. The best balance between internal and external focused organisations is to be found in applications. These are the market sub-segments, rather than the markets themselves, which tend to be too big and diverse to be practical markers for organisational structure. There are other organisational challenges to be faced, particularly around reporting lines and the whole question of managers versus management. Nick Obolensky explores this very well with his complex adaptive leadership model. Some progressive companies are doing away with manager roles altogether and letting teams self-manage themselves.

3) Culture and providing the right environment for collaboration – the "people" side of change and innovation is essential in getting the successful outcome that will help any business turn technology into profit – delivering new products that customers want and for which they are willing to pay a premium. Many behavioural barriers to achievement of such aims exist. They exist in our own mind as mental constructs and influence our behaviour in a negative way. Others with whom we work will experience barriers as well, many of which are the same but often different and difficult to understand. We hear ourselves and others giving voice to fears and concerns in relation to new ideas, and these hold us and the business back. Having a structured approach to identifying and working towards removing such barriers is key. The aim must be to build a positive mindset, not only in the leadership but at all levels of people in the business, to ensure they all understand they have a responsibility to be part of the creative process from ideas to implementation and profit. For successful innovation, the role of leadership must be to inspire and engage and to create the right environment for change and innovation.

Earlier this year, I was speaking at an international ceramics conference. I was privileged to be invited to give the opening keynote speech, during which I gave my views on the "The State of the UK Advanced Ceramics Market". But in addition, on day two of the conference, I also gave a presentation on the subject of this very book, entitled, "Transforming Advanced Materials Technologies into Profit – The Biggest Barrier to Innovation Is Your Own Business". Over 30 minutes, I summarised the key points that form the basis of this book. Afterwards, during the questions, one of the members of the audience stood up and asked me about the "culture" aspect of my presentation. In fact, what he said was more of a comment than a question. He told me that he accepted the point of the importance of culture in oiling the wheels of innovation in a business, and then he proceeded to explain about how he used to work in a business that had a toxic culture (actually the word he used was "polluted" culture) and that really prevented him from achieving anything, and he was very unhappy with his job. So he left and went to another business, where he claimed there was a much more positive culture and he was far happier. I guess the point he was trying to make was: yes, culture is a critical factor, but you don't necessarily have to work to change it as an individual, you can just move to another business and find a better culture to work within. I couldn't really fault his logic.

It is true that as an individual, as an employee, absolutely you have the right and the choice to move on to another job. But what it did remind me was how different things look depending on where you sit in an organisation. If you're a technician, a technical manager, a process engineer, a new business development executive, a CEO or the owner, your perspective is inevitably different. But don't forget, whatever your role, you're all looking at the same business.

The guy's comment reminded me that it's all very well for me to preach at the end of a 30-year career about how things work in an organisation. I have the comfort of not having to prove anything to anyone. I have stepped off the corporate ladder. I have paid my dues, done my time and am now reaping the rewards of a comfortable life (all earned by hard work of course!). But I do remember how it feels when you're in the middle of it all, when you need your job to pay your mortgage, to feed and clothe your family, when you don't have a safety net of savings in the bank to fall back on. I remember all those things, and I remember it is not a nice feeling to be so dependent, not having freedom from financial worries, but most of us have to go through this. And in such situations, as an employee, when the stakes are so high, people rarely want to rock the boat, rarely want to stick their head up and point out the problems in a business. I don't know the particular circumstances of the gentleman from the conference, but I assume he was like most of us, he needed his job, his income and couldn't risk shaking up the polluted culture in his old business, so he chose a lower risk strategy and changed his situation. I'm not sure how he could be confident he wasn't just moving into another toxic environment, but I guess from the way he described his situation, he was willing to take that chance. So I understand that it is not always an easy thing to make changes to your business structure and culture – even if you're the CEO – but the first step must be understanding that there is a problem, and having a structured approach to identifying where the problems are and how to deal with them. And this is the very reason I wrote this book, to help people through this challenge.

I wrote *Cracking the Innovation Code* to provide a playbook for people in industry to help them see the bigger picture, to help them identify where and what the barriers are to new product development in their business and to give them the tools to deal with them. Hopefully, wherever you sit in the organisation, however empowered you do or don't feel, having this book as a third party, independent reference point, and using the methodology described in it to help you create a detailed plan of action of organisational and cultural improvement is, I hope, a way of empowering everybody. So you don't have to necessarily stick your neck out and risk your job anymore, please feel free to wave this book in front of your boss and I can do that for you.

CONCLUSION

A CONVERSATION WITH MAURITS VAN TOL

As I came to the end of writing this book, I was considering the best way to bring all of the themes that we have covered together, in a way that is both memorable and helpful. In trawling my own career memories to add some examples and case studies to try to bring to life the many aspects of how organisation and culture impact a company's ability to innovate and grow through new products, one of the things I did was to discuss many of these examples, and the overarching themes, with several like-minded professionals, many of whom are listed in the acknowledgments. Being able to get direct feedback on your thoughts, ideas and management techniques from those you admire and trust is an extremely valuable gift, and one that has helped me to refine and clarify the concepts that form the foundation for this book. Whilst the feedback I received was from a range of professionals, experienced in a range of different disciplines, from operations, business management, sales, and many others, I also deliberately sought out a few key individuals who, like me, have had a career leading innovation in large corporations, blended with direct business management P&L roles. These are the people that I anticipated would have developed a unique perspective in their careers on how technology works within a business, and understand best how to extract real value from it to fuel business growth. Such individuals are quite rare, so I feel privileged to know a few such people with whom I can bounce ideas and concepts around. In particular, in having such conversations, I was hoping not only to solidify and reaffirm my own thoughts, but also to add further colour to the narrative, to try to ensure that the book was not just the product of a single voice. I was very fortunate that several of these discussions helped to add a handful of case studies and useful quotes to the book, which have ended up dispersed throughout these pages, but one conversation in particular turned into something which I felt could usefully become the closing section of this book, and form an effective wrap-up of many of the major themes we have explored.

In exploring the themes of this book with Maurits van Tol, I was very lucky to be able to have the chance to compare and contrast his thoughts with my own experience. At the time of writing (December 2019), Maurits, a Dutch national, has recently been appointed as the new Chief Technology Officer at Johnson Matthey, the £14 billion–turnover British multinational speciality chemicals and sustainable technologies company, which is listed on the London Stock Exchange as part of the FTSE 100 Index. Prior to this, Maurits held senior leadership roles at two other large multi-national chemical and industrial products manufacturers: first at DSM, as Global Marketing Director, Business Manager and Vice-President R&D of a variety of business divisions, and more recently at the Borealis Group, where he was Senior Vice President Innovation and Technology.

Our dialogue proved to be a catalyst for Maurits to think about his own approach to tackling the challenge of unlocking a company's ability to create value and growth from technology. The list he came up with struck me as a masterclass in the key things to consider when starting in a new company to address the structural and cultural challenges of unlocking innovation and to grow the business through new products, and resonated heavily with the themes I have explored in this book. His list very much supports my own approach and the things I have written about in this book, but also adds some new points of view from Maurits' own experience. In particular, Maurits' list reflects his own practical mindset, an approach that I very much share and advocate, and one that I feel is too lacking in much of the innovation literature available these days, and was the main reason I started writing these books in the first place. There is far too much innovation advice out there today, much of which is too academic, overtly complex and potentially confusing to make it of practical value in a real business environment. Unless you have been directly responsible for delivering business growth yourself, unless you have worked for many years creating new technologies and delivering new products to the market place, working with real teams, across multiple market landscapes, experiencing both successes and failures, it is difficult for anyone to truly understand the practical challenges of making it all work, and Maurits is one of those guys who has been there and done it. And therefore, I felt Maurits' list would form an excellent summary and conclusion to this book.

Maurits acknowledges that when you first step into a new company, there are hundreds of things you can try to change in order to transform it into one that can better grow through innovation and new products, but if you want to make a real tangible impact, you need to start by focusing on just three to five of the most important and make those happen. The following are the top five things that he has learnt to start with, ranked in order of importance:

1) Tone from the Top – the culture of any company is set by the people at the top. Maurits has developed and presented his views on this a number of times in a presentation he calls "Tone from the Top". What he has learnt over time is that if the leadership team are not able to role model the behaviours and values they preach, then all their presentations and communications, and all their words designed to set and influence the tone of the business culture, are just empty air, and people will see through them immediately. If a CEO states that innovation is important to a business, if they say that technology, R&D and all the other aspects of innovation are critical to the growth of the business, then they had better mean it. They have to be able to deliver effectively in an elevator speech that R&D is truly important to them and to the business, otherwise it just will not work. Maurits learnt all this from previous roles, earlier in his career, where he found himself working within environments where R&D was looked at purely as a cost, and discovered that in such cases, without support from the top, it simply cannot and will not be successful. On one occasion, later on in his career, when he was offered a new senior role in a new company, before he was even prepared to accept the job, he first went to the boss and explained that R&D cannot just be "tolerated", the boss needs to consider R&D as an important and vital aspect of the future of the company, and to support him directly, otherwise there was no

point in him taking the job, because he knew he would be setting himself up for failure. Over time, he learnt that CEOs, presidents, and other people at the top of an organisation, have not generally been exposed to or worked in the area of innovation, or in a company in which innovation was core, and so do not appreciate the role they play in driving a business forward, and this is where the origin of the "R&D as a cost" attitude comes from. And more than this, in order to make innovation successful in any business, Maurits has come to understand that the CEO and the CTO have to buddy up and form a double act, because this becomes central in successfully setting the "Tone from the Top" required to lead the business to growth through new product development.

2) Organisational structure and managing the interfaces – in his 30-year career, Maurits has worked in almost every type of business structure, ranging from highly corporate-centric, to highly decentralised, with multiple autonomous sites. And his experience has demonstrated to him that there is no ideal structure, because everything can work and everything can fail. During his time at Borealis, the business was structured into global divisions, and his role was such that he was the boss of all things related to polyethylene technology worldwide, including the intellectual property and technology licensing departments. But he recognised that he still needed support from other business units within the group to get things done, and this was where he learnt that collaboration between disciplines like sales and marketing, operations and R&D has to work seamlessly. At DSM, the organisation was much more scattered, with all the different businesses having a lot of autonomy. In his new role at Johnson Matthey, he is again discovering an organisation that is also very scattered, with lots of sub-units having their own CEOs and sub-organisations, but the key positive he has found is that despite any structural and geographical splits, there is a true willingness to work together that pervades the whole organisation, and that is the key to success that he has observed over the years. What Maurits has learnt is that it is not so much the structure that matters, it is how you manage the interfaces within that structure that is more important. When joining any new business, you first need to spend some time to recognise the structure that is in place and then work at connecting all the dots. This requires a large

amount of communication time, to identify and build bridges with those at the interfaces of the organisation. He has not observed any direct link between the type of structure and the nature of the interfaces, and has found that all models can work if you take time to recognise and manage effectively the interfaces. He feels confident in his ability to work in any organisational setup, just as long as things are clear, such as reporting lines and boundaries. To make things clear, Maurits has found that having well-defined, explicit job descriptions is extremely important. The very act of forcing people to sit down, discuss, agree and write such things down together is essential in achieving this. Once the job description is locked down, Maurits is happy to put it in a drawer and never look at it again, because it is having the dialogue and writing it down that makes the difference and sets the boundaries.

3) Focusing the project portfolio – during his time at Borealis, his peers claimed that one of the biggest impacts that Maurits had on the business was bringing his approach to focusing the project portfolio, and significantly reducing the number of projects they were trying to work on. He recognised that if you have 200 projects going on, it is just not possible to focus on and deliver them all. His approach in any new business now is to review the project portfolio, decide on those projects which will have the biggest impact, and work to bring down the number of main projects and programmes to between five and seven. This allows the whole of the management of the company to be clear on what the project priorities are, which in turn elevates the importance of these projects, and makes sure everyone is focused on the same set of key projects. Having a smaller number of key projects results in a smaller number of multi-disciplinary steering groups that bring the necessary disciplines together. And bringing these people together every month for one or two hours on a call ensures they all have an important role to play and helps to manage the interfaces more effectively.

4) Having a relentless discipline in execution – in tandem with the approach to focusing the new business project portfolio down to only five to seven main projects and programmes, in order to make sure that these fewer projects actually get delivered, Maurits also ensures that each project has a high-level steering team, composed of those

gatekeepers who can make things happen within the organisation. This team acts as the oil in the machine, helping to cut through the barriers that any project inevitably encounters from time to time as it progresses. And to maintain high-level focus and involvement at the very top, progress on these key projects are reported at each supervisory board meeting, using the reporting discipline of a simple dashboard containing a system of traffic light progress against key targets and milestones. This ensures the projects become ultra-official, and well known and understood by all in the top team. In addition, progress is further incentivised for the CEO, and members of the business management team, by having some element of their annual bonus linked to project progress. All these disciplines help to further develop "tone from the top", and help the business "move fast and get things done".

5) One owner, one accountable person in the company – another key element that Maurits has learnt is vital in achieving business success from technology is ensuring that each part of any business has one clear owner for all things technology, one person who is accountable. And that means at each level of the business, at individual sites, at regional or divisional level and at board level, however the business is structured. During his time at Borealis, it was widely understood that anything new came to him as the CTO. If the company believes that technology is important to the company, it should have one key individual who has an overview of the technology platforms that will make a difference, and in his new role as CTO at Johnson Matthey, again, he has oversight of everything that's going on technologically. Having such a role at each and every level of a company, be it technical manager, technical director or whatever, provides a focal point for innovation at each site and within the whole business. Also important, is making sure that everyone in the business understands the nature of these roles and where the appropriate responsibilities and accountabilities lie. That way, the roles are respected and can be given the freedom to work within the business structure and culture. When it comes to lines of communication and reporting structures, these will differ with different organisational models. In Maurits' current role, the site and divisional technology roles have a dotted-line reporting relationship with his CTO role, and this was explicit as

> part of his job description when he took on the role. Maurits accepts that dotted-line reporting will always be weaker than solid lines, but the success of any reporting relationship always depends on how the line manager behaves and on having clear guidelines of protocol. For example, Johnson Matthey have a protocol that says whenever a new technical manager is hired at the site level, the site management should involve Maurits, as CTO, in the process. And so far, in his first few months in the role, this has happened twice, so he is confident that there are rules in place and that everyone follows and respects them – yet another example that has impressed Maurits with the culture of collaboration he sees in Johnson Matthey.

One of the key messages I feel that Maurits' list of the top five things he has learnt through his career about how to realign a business to better grow through innovation and new products, is that it shows how clear, practical approaches make the biggest impact. Each of the five approaches are simple, understandable by all, and can be achieved with the introduction of minimal new business processes and reporting mechanisms. But that is not to say they are all easy to make happen. Much of the secret behind the successful implementation of these five items is down to the influencing skills of the technology lead, coupled with a high degree of empathy and a heavy dose of diplomacy, both in the boardroom, and throughout the whole business. Having a clear set of guidelines to work towards is a wonderful first step, and the list should help up-and-coming technology professionals in many industries with a plan of action, but in reality you are only likely to get there by growing your maturity, building your experience and by working on your EQ.

I was extremely pleased and felt immensely privileged to have been able to have this in-depth exchange with Maurits, especially at a time when he is very busy with his big new job. For me, it validated many things that I had been writing about, echoing many of the key themes, not only of this book, but also in my previous business book *Transforming Technology into Profit*, and ultimately it made me realise that I am not alone in experiencing the challenges that I have faced during my corporate career. It can be no coincidence that number one on Maurits' list, is the importance of getting the leadership fully aligned, and his "tone From the top" approach echoes my own experiences, which I captured at the end of Chapter 2, in "Why Do Businesses Struggle to Grow through New Products? It All Starts at the Top". The critical need to recognise and manage the functional interfaces within an organisation is a subject I return to again and again in my books, particularly in Chapter 2 of this book, so it was gratifying to hear it also formed a key part of Maurits' philosophy. The importance of identifying the key priorities in a business' project portfolio, and focusing the management team on delivering just these forms the next level of Maurits' approach. The importance of portfolio management to maximise the likelihood of delivering those projects which will deliver the biggest impact, is something I wrote about extensively in Chapter 6 of *Transforming Technology into Profit*.

As Maurits explained his views to me on the final item on his list – exploring accountability, ownership and reporting lines – I was reminded of an experiment in reorganisation I tried in my last big corporate role as CTO. In taking on this role, I walked into a traditionally structured global multi-national, one based mostly around geographical regions. We had a hybrid structure of North America, South America, Europe, and Asia reporting regions, plus a stand-alone global business unit, each with a managing director, and each with its own board of directors, covering the usual functions: sales, operations, finance, technology, human resources, etc. In terms of reporting lines, I had in previous companies experienced the situation that Maurits described, where my role was leading technology and innovation at the central corporate board level, with individual business units having their own local structures, with a full suite of functional management roles, and in such circumstances, I had always had dotted-line reporting to me with respect to the local technology leads. Whilst Maurits has explained that this can work perfectly well if other things are in place, I had in some of my own earlier roles found myself in a less mature work environment, where there was not the same degree of collaborative attitude and universal understanding of structure and accountability, which created a number of barriers to developing new ideas and transforming them into successful new products, many of which I wrote about in my previous business book.

Because my own experience of dotted-line reporting structures had been one that led to significant challenges in delivery, I decided in my next big role to reverse the whole situation and got agreement from each of the regional managing directors that the regional technical directors should report to me directly instead. This was a significant departure from the traditional hierarchy that had been in place in the business throughout its history and took a lot of one-on-one time with all the stakeholders to explain all the changes, and the reasoning behind them. What I wanted to achieve by doing this was to raise the profile of the technology function within the business, and to achieve a joined-up set of resources that could collaborate more directly on those projects and that would deliver the biggest impact to the global business. Prior to this restructuring, the new business development project portfolio had naturally prioritised regional and local projects, because these were the ones that looked the most attractive and relevant to the local businesses. Any big global strategic projects were treated as something to get round to once all the local projects had been done, which for practical purposes meant that trying to progress on any of the big collaborative projects was almost impossible. One of the barriers that you encounter when trying to put together a global team is that the administration of people's payroll, tax, health benefits, etc. have to be done locally. But don't let such practical issues stand in the way of what you believe is the right thing to do, all such things can be dealt with.

Once we had the global team in place, this naturally led to a reversal of priorities, and meant that the small number of big global priority projects, those with the largest impact on the global business, became the new focus for the business, and reporting mechanisms were set up that kept these as high profile subjects on every board meeting agenda. Taking technology global also led to a closer communication and collaboration with the sales teams through the joint building of a global customer relationship management system. Within two years, across the whole of the global business, we doubled the new business opportunity pipeline, doubled the rate of conversion of new business opportunities and delivered an increase in new product sales of around 150%. So, with a dedicated team, an understanding management willing to try new things, and the enthusiasm to work hard to join all the dots, it is absolutely possible to utilise new technology to deliver real business growth.

It certainly feels good to have found a like-minded individual in Maurits that I can talk to, and I look forward to many more conversations with him. And this encounter reinforces my view that you cannot work all of this stuff out by yourself in isolation. Throughout your own career journey, you jump from one work situation to another, sometimes planned, sometimes a crisis, as things hit you that were impossible to see coming. Amongst all the daily turbulence, the continuous demands of work are such that it is difficult to stop and set aside some thinking time to make sense of what you have learnt along the way. You certainly get a sense, a feeling, of what and how things are happening along the way, how the way the company is organised, how your working relationships, and how the attitudes and culture of a work place all affect what you are trying to achieve, but not usually in any way that you can formulate a clear and communicable model. Having good quality conversations with other professionals is a vital part in helping you to do that, and beyond that, I have discovered that sitting down to plan and write a book is the ultimate way in which to make sense of it all. It forces you to have that thinking time, to build an understanding of what you have experienced, and to crystallise it into simple concepts, ideas and conclusions that you can pass on to the next generation, so that they don't have to go through the at times painful learning experiences that you did. That is what I have hoped to achieve with these books, and I thank each and every one of my collaborators, not only the ones named within the text or those listed in the acknowledgements, but also those countless others, whose points of view, whose feedback and comments throughout my career, have all in their own way contributed to what you are reading today.

So finally, thank you for reading this book. I hope that it has helped you to understand better the complex nature of how businesses work when it comes to trying to create new products and to appreciate better what things are important and what are just distractions. Wherever your business is in its innovation maturity journey, know that there are always improvements to be made, always a next level to aspire to, and hopefully this book has given you some practical guidance on how to get there.

Good luck,

Andy

For Product Safety Concerns and Information please contact our EU representative GPSR@taylorandfrancis.com
Taylor & Francis Verlag GmbH, Kaufingerstraße 24, 80331 München, Germany

www.ingramcontent.com/pod-product-compliance
Ingram Content Group UK Ltd.
Pitfield, Milton Keynes, MK11 3LW, UK
UKHW011015180926
475701UK00004B/752

9780367567118